THE VEIL OF CHAOS

living with weather

ALONG THE BRITISH COLUMBIA COAST

OWEN S. LANGE

acknowledgements

Lloyd's Acts was the first Marine Insurance available for Shipping Companies. The underwriting members of Lloyd's was initiated in 1871 under the direction of Admiral Paulsey.

This book was written with the support of many people. Below is a listing of those who played an active role in the creation, though not always directly. To them I give my heartfelt thanks. There were many others who provided ideas and inspiration behind the scenes.

My first thanks must go to the National Search and Rescue Secretariat who provided much of the financial support for this book. Without them this book would not have been possible.

I would then like to thank all those who spoke with me about BC coastal weather during these last two years. They are the ones who have experienced first-hand all the varieties of weather described in this book. A listing of their names is found in the Appendix.

During my trips along the coast doing research for this book I travelled in three different types of vessels. The first was on a 37 foot sailboat, the *Kabirian*, which took me as far north as Klemtu. I would like to thank Peter Lange who ably skippered the boat; Christophe Grieve, the seaman and cook; and Ann McLennon, who allowed her boat to be used. The BC ferry *Queen of the North* (Capt. Ken Wright) took me to Prince Rupert, and the *Queen of Prince Rupert* (Capt. Ted Raynor) to the Queen Charlotte Islands. Two coastal steamers, *The Lady Rose*, with Capt. Raif Moss, took me into Barkley Sound, and the *Uchuck III* with Capt. Fred Mather and Sean Mather took me from Gold River to Tahsis and Zeballos.

Mert Horita, Laurie Neil, Colin di Cenzo, and Pat Wong formed the editing team. Judy Kwan and Dawn Andrews helped with mapping issues. Dick Boak gave graphical advice.

Thanks also to the graphic design firm of Butler + Wood Design for their graphics and layout, and to Wiet Wildeman for the diagonal line drawings in Chapter 1.

The synthetic aperture radar (SAR) derived wind images in Chapter 3 were kindly made available by the Johns Hopkins University Applied Physics Laboratory, and the NOAA/NESDIS Ocean Remote Sensing Program's Alaska SAR Demonstration. The Canadian Space Agency was the source of the original RADARSAT-1 Synthetic Aperture Radar Data that was processed by the Alaska SAR Facility of the University of Alaska, Fairbanks.

Final thanks go to my wife, Marilyn, my daughter Rosie, and friends who provided support when I was too stressed to do anything beyond the book.

table of contents

preface

In our life on earth we continually breathe in air from the atmosphere around us, then moments later breathe it out again. We live within the atmosphere of the earth. The movements of air around and above us create forms that dance unseen, until they express themselves in ever-changing clouds and weather. In our breathing we live within these forms, within the weather - we are in truth, weathermen, weatherwomen. Living with weather is not an option, it is part of life. This is most keenly experienced in our coastal communities where many aspects of daily life are directly affected by the changes of weather around us. Becoming aware of these changes, and understanding how and why they happen, is the purpose of this book, *Living with weather*.

The book has four main parts. The first chapter, "Weather imagination," attempts to provide a way of "seeing" weather that goes beyond simple facts so that an inner picture, or imagination, of the processes can be created. The second chapter, "Weather systems," provides information on how weather systems develop and move across the offshore waters, and how the conditions associated with them change when the coast is encountered. The third chapter, "The four winds," looks at the general weather patterns across the coast with the aid of satellite pictures and weather maps. The fourth chapter, "Regional weather guides" gives detailed information about the winds, waves, and weather for all parts of the coast, in all seasons of the year. Reference materials are found in the "Appendix."

The occasional personal comment is written in blue type. Quotes that give memorable wording to some of the ideas appear in the sidebars. Interesting anecdotes, coastal trivia, and more technical comments are in shaded boxes.

This book cannot hope to discuss all aspects of coastal weather, but is only one part of a lifelong learning process. Keeping a log of your own observations will help that process. Before travelling, check out other books such as *Sailing Directions* and listen to the knowledge of local mariners. Remember that tides are often as important to consider as the weather. Take both into account as you plan your day, and move according to nature, not by the clock. Enjoy the many wonders of the British Columbia coast. Weather is a big part of this experience.

weather imagination

EXPERIENCING THE PHENOMENA OF WEATHER

EXPERIENCING THE PHENOMENA OF WEATHER

WEATHER, MORE THAN ANYTHING ELSE, IS A PROCESS - a process of becoming, through the stream of time. This process can be seen in the daily changes of sun, clouds and wind, and in the cycle of the year.

Through the years I have found that many people are able to learn facts about weather, but still do not feel that they understand it. Because of this I have tried an approach not found in most other books. I have tried to go beyond a listing of simple facts, and instead have tried to build a picture, or imagination, of the ever-moving and transforming nature of the atmosphere. The hope is that from this, you will be able to create your own picture, into which the many individual facts about weather will find their place.

"Imagination is more important than knowledge."
ALBERT EINSTEIN

The atmosphere is so vast and has such an interconnected weaving of its movements that more than one approach is necessary to view it all. As a result three different perspectives are considered. The first looks at weather from the vantage point of what we, from our earthly perspective, can observe. By seeing the many phenomena that make up weather, by taking note of their many changes, we can learn from the phenomena themselves. Since the act of observing is in itself a way of knowing, it is important for you to make your own observations, for they are the ones that will open up the deepest understanding.

The second perspective involves seeing the atmosphere as one part of a global, and even cosmic system, in which many elements interweave. The atmosphere does not exist in isolation. The four elements, earth, water, air, and warmth, are all affected by influences from beyond the earth, from the cosmos. The most noticeable effects on the earth-ocean-atmosphere system come from the sun, but the moon also plays its part. The third perspective is time. Weather, more than anything else, is a process - a process of becoming, through the stream of time. This process can be seen on many levels, but is most evident in the cycle of the year, in the four seasons.

The west coast of BC has such an abundance of weather that it is sometimes called the "raincoast," or "wet coast."

"There is something that I don't understand," said Billy Proctor, of Echo Bay, as I walked into his house, hardly before I had the chance to take off my coat. "Over on Cox Island - I've seen it many times - when you get strong northwest winds - it's clear - but there is a cap of fog on top of Cox Island. It stays there, but is blowing like hell." Billy, like all good observers of nature, ponders the meanings of things he does not understand. His question is a good one, for the phenomena he witnessed sum up some basic things about weather. The "cap of fog," as he called it, can be seen on many mountaintops across the coast - if the conditions are right. But what are the conditions? To find an answer to this, and hopefully to other questions as well, we need to step back and look at the basic features of our ever-changing weather.

Have you ever been to a desert, either the desert of the southern BC interior, or the vast deserts of north Africa and the Middle East? Have you experienced the hot sun beating down on a parched landscape? The air is still, silent, and invisible. There seems to be nothing between you and the sun. Except for the yellow-brown haze that blurs the horizon, everything is sharp and clear, just like the crystalline sands beneath your feet.

Compare this picture with a rainy winter day on the BC coast. The sun is forgotten. Rain fills the sky and hides all but a hint of the clouds above. Distant mountains disappear, and nearby landmarks fade in the surrounding veil of mist. Wind rattles the rigging, rain beats on the roof, and waves crash on the shore. The boat pitches back and forth with every gust. Everything is wet, moving, and blaring.

The main difference between these two pictures is the presence of water. Not just the water of the ocean, and the water that falls from the clouds, but also the water that does its transforming trick, and vanishes into the air when the clouds break and the sun returns. Deserts appear to have no weather, while the west coast of BC has such an abundance of weather that it is sometimes called the "raincoast," or "wet coast." Water is truly the key to weather. It could be said that weather *is* water. The two words, weather and water, even have similar linguistic origins.

Water

About 70% of the earth's surface is water. Water takes on the shape of whatever container that holds it - be it a drinking glass or an ocean basin. But on its own, it takes the shape of a sphere, as seen in a dewdrop on the grass, or the raindrop that forms on the shiny surface of painted woodwork. It is transparent in its pure state, but since it can dissolve most other substances, it usually has other elements within it, which give it its colour. Water is at its most dense condition, not when it is solid, for ice is lighter than water, but when it is a liquid, at 4°C. Because of this, ocean bottoms are never colder than 4°C, and hence, the oceans do not freeze from the bottom up.

But of all water's properties, the one that is most important for weather is its ability to change between a solid, a liquid, and a gas. It is the only substance that can do this, within the normal temperature ranges of the earth. And if this is not special enough, water has the ability to absorb heat from the surrounding environment when it transforms from ice to liquid water, or from a liquid to a gas, with very little change to its own temperature. Likewise, its temperature changes little when it releases this heat again as it changes from a gas to a liquid, or from a liquid to a solid. This ability to store heat and to transfer it, as it moves around the earth, is a big part of the energy system that drives the weather processes.

Water is the element that is transformed. But the heat from the sun is the transformer. Warmth is invisible to the eye, but pervades everything. The degree of warmth varies from place to place and through time. Warmth is not only the transformer of water but is also the source of most movements of air and water. Movement, in its turn, transports air in such ways that it brings about further heating or cooling. Air movement is thus intimately connected with the transformation of the water that it carries, from one state to another. If the movement of air is thought of as wind, then weather can be seen as the weaving of water, warmth, and wind.

Movement of air and water

Billy Proctor, when describing the cap cloud, said the wind was "blowing like hell." Moving air can be heard and felt, but cannot be seen. What is seen is either something moving in the wind, or something affected by the force of the wind. The bending of trees, the raising of waves on the sea, and the cap cloud are all results, the visible expressions, of wind. Another way to visualize the

On its own, water takes the shape of a sphere, as seen in a dewdrop on the grass.

3

movement of air is to study the movements of water. Slow-moving air takes on no forms. The movements appear random and chaotic. The smoke from an extinguished candle drifts and turns with no apparent form or structure. But when air moves more rapidly then it will develop wave like forms, vortices will be created, and boundaries will develop within the flow. Fast-moving air moves like water.

Movement with a flowing stream

Many phenomena of water movement can be seen in the flowing of a small stream. If it is not possible to actually sit down beside a river and watch its movements, bring it alive in your imagination. The first thing you will notice is that the water flows fast in the middle, but at the edge it flows slowly and may even be lapping backward against the flow. The faster water glides past the slower moving water near the bank. If the water flows past an obstacle such as a rock or tree trunk, a part of the water flow is blocked. The water that flows past the obstacle undergoes shearing, and creates a vortex, or more likely, a train of vortices, that move with the flowing stream, slowly weakening and dissipating as they travel farther downstream.

The water flows fast in the middle, but at the edge it flows slowly and may even be lapping backward against the flow.

Hard and soft boundaries

When two streams with somewhat different characteristics meet, a boundary is formed between them. This can be seen where the Fraser River enters the southern Strait of Georgia. A distinct line marking the boundary between the two waters persists well beyond the mouth of the river and at times almost reaches the Gulf Islands. Waves can be seen along this boundary. A similar boundary can be seen where the Thompson and Fraser rivers come together near Lytton, BC. The clear Thompson water contrasts with the muddy Fraser water. The boundary between these two flows oscillates back and forth, and waves develop along it. The solid edge of a riverbank forms a "hard" boundary for the moving stream. The boundary between two moving streams is "soft" by comparison, but both produce similar types of movements.

Soft boundaries can move, transform in shape, and even disappear, while hard boundaries remain stationary and unchanging. Soft boundaries are generally caused by differences in density between two fluid streams, which in turn are primarily caused by variations in temperature. They can also arise from differences in water content, and even from differences in speeds of motion within the fluid. The soft boundary is only in existence because two streams of fluid are moving toward one another. The weather feature called a "front," which is described later, is the classic example of such a boundary.

Progressive and stationary waves

The running stream exhibits three types of movement: flowing, shearing, and rotating. From these motions, vortices are formed. Observation of the river also reveals another waterform, namely waves. Two types of waves can be observed in moving waters. The first type occurs when the wave moves and the water remains almost stationary. This is called a progressive wave. Ocean wind waves are progressive waves. The water in a progressive wave actually moves in circles or ellipses but does not move forward with the waveform. A bird sitting on the wave will be seen to move in backward circles as the waveform moves under it. The waveform can cross the entire ocean but the water itself remains more or less where it is.

The second type of wave occurs when the water moves, but the waveform remains almost stationary. This is called a stationary wave and is seen in the form created by water steadily flowing over a rock in a river. Another example of a stationary wave is the meandering river. The snake-like waveform of the river can be seen from a plane, or on a map, but through this waveform the water streams onward. The jet stream is another example, for it is a large wave that moves eastward around the globe, and within it move winds of up to 200 knots. So even though the form of the jet stream slowly changes over time, it can be viewed from this perspective, as a stationary wave. Frontal waves and moving lows can also be seen in the same light - they are waveforms through which winds move.

"When you make the finding yourself - even if you're the last person on earth to see the light - you'll never forget it."

CARL SAGAN

As a light breeze begins to blow over water, small, darkened, ruffled patches, called cats-paws appear. Waves on the ocean, generally called ocean waves, or wind waves, develop with the winds. When the winds stop, the waves that develop from these winds don't immediately die, but continue moving onward in the general direction of the winds. In time, as the waves move farther away from where they were formed, they stretch out into longer waves with more gentle slopes. These waves, which migrate away from the area where they were formed, are called swell waves, or simply swell. The steepness of swell waves is much lower than a wind wave of a similar height.

Clouds

The sun has just risen. It had been raining most of the night. The clouds have broken to allow a shaft of light to shine on the still wet leaves of a laurel hedge. Rising from the leaves are wafts of vapour, which disappear again a short distance above. The leaves of the plants farther down the hedge, which are outside the shaft of light, show no tendrils of rising vapours. Are they there, but need the light to be seen? Or are the wafts of vapour only there because of the light?

The sky continues to clear as the morning progresses. The air has a fresh smell of newly watered earth. Smells are always more intense in humid air. The blue sky is shinier and brighter blue than on recent days. A small white cloud appears above the nearby hill but disappears again as the sun rises higher. Another cloud appears somewhat later and begins to grow and fill the sky. The cloud rises up and forms a cauliflower shaped top. The once fluffy white cloud is now dark, and threatening rain. The rain begins, first lightly but then with torrential strength. Strong, gusty winds shake the nearby trees. As suddenly as it began, the cloud moves off and a band of light streams in across the late afternoon sky. A rainbow, no, two rainbows, one much fainter than the other, arc across the dark horizon. Rivulets of water course across the ground and flow back into the ocean. Within a few hours the entire cycle of water that is seen above the earth has taken place.

Rising from the leaves are wafts of vapour, which disappear again a short distance above.

Clouds are transformation indicators. They are the result of water being changed from an invisible gas into a visible droplet of liquid water, or to crystals of ice. The water is there before and after the transformation, but is only seen when in the liquid or solid state. A transformation back into an invisible gas occurs as the cloud breaks up and disappears. A cloud is the visible expression of the presence of water in the air. It is also an expression of air movement. If air moves upward it expands due to having less air above it, and cools with the expansion. This cooling allows the water vapour to condense into a liquid. The capacity for air to hold water as a vapour changes with the temperature. If it moves downward it comes under greater pressure and is warmed so that the water vapour transforms back into an invisible gas.

The names of clouds

Clouds come in a wide variety of shapes. Each shape indicates the type of air movement that is occurring. An understanding of movement is needed to understand the formation and types of clouds. Many people over the centuries have named and classified the clouds, but it was Luke Howard, in 1802, who gave them names that have stuck, and have been in use ever since. He described three basic cloud forms: cirrus, stratus, and cumulus, and to these he added a fourth, nimbus, for rain bearing clouds. Modern science has combined the three basic types into the subtypes shown on the accompanying cloud triangle. Clouds have also been classified from an aviation perspective based on their height above ground, into low, middle, and high clouds.

Luke Howard's classification system has three basic cloud forms. Several others have been added between them.

A slight modification of Luke Howard's classification system yields three basic cloud forms: layered, vertical and mixed. The layered clouds are flat, relatively featureless clouds that sometimes extend to the horizon and beyond. When this cloud covers vast areas over the earth's surface it creates an enclosing gesture around the earth. All stratus, altostratus, and cirrostratus clouds fit into this type. The vertical clouds, such as the cumulus and cumulonimbus, extend to various heights straight upward away from the earth. The third, mixed type has vertical development and also extends over larger horizontal areas. Stratocumulus, altocumulus, and cirrocumulus are in this mixed group.

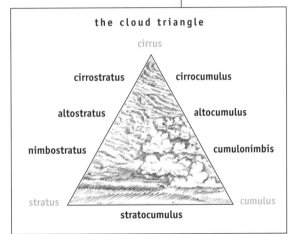

the cloud triangle

cirrus

cirrostratus **cirrocumulus**

altostratus **altocumulus**

nimbostratus **cumulonimbis**

stratus cumulus

stratocumulus

Stratocumulus clouds

The stratocumulus cloud is the most common cloud in our skies. It could be viewed as the archetypal cloud, for it expresses many of the motions found in the atmosphere. It is a layered cloud, but has distinctive rolling elements that give the impression of it having a bubbling circulation within it, which in fact, it does. It is a boundary phenomenon, for it forms between an area of drier subsiding air above, and an area of moist, rising air below. Winds blow steadily through the layer.

Stratocumulus clouds can form after the passage of a front, for the rain that accompanied the front has added moisture to the lower layers of air, and the sun that appears after the clouds have cleared, heats the ground. The air near the ground warms and begins to rise upward. The invisible water vapour

The stratocumulus cloud gives the impression of having a bubbling circulation within it.

**CLOUD
ELEMENT GUIDE**

---

cirrocumulus
*one finger wide
(at arm's length)*

altocumulus
two fingers wide

stratocumulus
*more than
two fingers wide*

changes into water droplets and cumulus type clouds are formed. But at the same time a ridge of higher pressure often builds in behind the frontal trough, and in this ridge, the air is subsiding. The subsiding air forms a cap to the vertical motion and spreads out the moisture in the layer. A rolling, bubbling motion develops in the flow within the layer. The air cools as it rises and warms again as it falls. The water vapour is changed into water droplets as it cools and changes back into invisible water vapour in the warming, descending motion. These bubbling motions spread throughout the layer.

Altocumulus clouds are formed in the same way as stratocumulus clouds but are called by a different name only because they are formed at a higher height in the atmosphere. There is no specifically defined height that determines if it is called a stratocumulus or altocumulus cloud but generally stratocumulus clouds are found below 7,000 feet, and they are called altocumulus if their bases are at least this value. The cloud roll elements appear smaller in the altocumulus because of their perspective of being higher but also because the bubbling process can be less vigorous at greater heights. Cirrocumulus clouds are again similar but in this case the main difference is that this cloud is made of ice crystals instead of water droplets. The cloud elements appear to be smaller than in the altocumulus due to greater distance from the ground observer.

Rain and drizzle

The motions within the clouds continually evolve and change. If the air is unstable and the upward motions are greater than the downward ones then the breaks between the elements of stratocumulus cloud shrink and the cloud spreads out into one larger cloud mass that may occupy much of the sky. If the downward motions are greater than the upward ones then the breaks between the cloud elements increase in size, and the roll cloud separates into individual cumulus clouds. Sometimes the cumulus clouds will build sufficiently to produce rain. Rain occurs when the water in the cloud combines into droplets that are big enough to overcome the rising air in the cloud, allowing them to fall earthward. If the upward currents of air are not strong, smaller water droplets will be able to fall out of the cloud. These smaller droplets are called drizzle. In very large cumulus clouds, with very strong updrafts of air, the water droplets need to grow quite large before they can overcome the upward currents.

Temperature, clouds, and weather

Clouds form when invisible water vapour changes into visible liquid water droplets, or solid ice crystals. Since the temperature of the atmosphere is generally colder at higher altitudes than at the surface the process of changing from water vapour to ice crystals is quite common. But at what temperature do ice crystals form? The normal answer would be at 0°C, but this is generally not the case. Ice melts and becomes a liquid at 0°C but liquid water does not necessarily change into a solid at this temperature. In most cases this transformation from a liquid to a solid requires something for the water to condense upon, called condensation nuclei. Sea salt acts as the condensation nuclei in most coastal areas. Without this, water may remain as a liquid until near -40°C. But this would only occur in pure air. In practice, however, the atmosphere has many potential condensation nuclei, so ice crystals form at a much warmer temperature, but even then normally not until at least -10°C. This fact allows rainbows to form with water droplets, even when the temperature is below freezing.

The temperature of the air beneath the cloud has an impact on the type of precipitation that falls from the cloud. Once the cloud droplets have amassed together sufficiently to overcome the upward motions in the cloud, they can begin to precipitate, or fall, out of the cloud. If the cloud is composed of water droplets then they will fall as rain if the temperature beneath the cloud is above freezing. If the temperature is below freezing they will either solidify into ice pellets, or will hit the ground as super-cooled water droplets and freeze instantly upon contact. The latter situation occurs if the depth of cold air, through which the droplets are falling, is not enough to freeze the droplets while in the air. If the cloud is composed of ice crystals they will fall as snow if the temperature beneath the cloud is below freezing, or will melt into rain if the air below the cloud is above freezing.

The temperature of the air beneath the cloud has an impact on the type of precipitation that falls from the cloud.
←

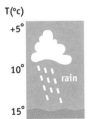
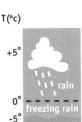
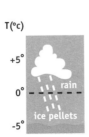
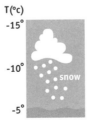
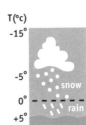

Hail

When a water droplet tries to fall out of the cloud but is not heavy enough to overcome the strong upward currents, it is carried back upward into the cloud. If the droplet rises to a level that has a temperature cold enough, it may freeze. Then once the frozen droplet becomes heavy enough to fall earthward it will partially melt as it falls through warmer air. But then it can be swept upward again in the strong upward currents. This process of up and down movement with repeated melting and freezing of the droplet, results in an onion-like, multi-layered object that eventually gains sufficient weight to fall right out of the cloud and hit the earth as "hail."

Fog

Temperature also plays a strong role in the formation of fog. Radiation fog forms over land late at night, as the land surface loses heat and the air near the ground is cooled enough for condensation to occur. The greatest cooling occurs with clear skies and light winds. Radiation fog usually occurs in thin layers over lower lying lands. It may drift over the water when light land breezes develop during the night but it rarely spreads far out to sea. Fog can also form over harbours and inlets, where cold air settles through drainage from the surrounding mountains. When this happens, however, the heat from the water usually warms the lowest layers of the fog so that it lifts into low stratus clouds.

Fog can form along the coast over harbours and inlets where cold air settles through drainage from the surrounding mountains.

Radiation fog is most common from late summer until late autumn, particularly after days of rainy weather. The fog burns off over the land after sunrise, but is slower to clear over the water. As the nights grow longer with the approach of winter, and the temperatures fall, the fog can begin earlier and can take longer to burn off.

Sea fog or advection fog is formed when warm moist air moves over colder sea water. The moisture in the air condenses into fog, the same way a person's warm breath condenses on a cold day. Unlike radiation fog, which requires calm or light wind conditions, sea fog may form when winds are moderate and may even persist as winds become strong. One mariner summed up the types of fog as follows: you get land fog (radiation fog) with warm water and cold land, and you get ocean fog with cold water and warm land. Because of these tempera-ture variations, land fog is most common in the late winter and early spring, when the land is coolest, and the water is relatively warm. Ocean or sea fog is most common in the late summer and early fall when the land is warm compared to the water. Land fog tends to come and go fairly quickly, while sea fog may sit over the water for days on end, with it spreading closer to the coast and into the inlets overnight, and moving off the coast with the heat of the day. In years in which the water is warmer than normal there will be less fog during the autumn. When the water is colder than normal the fog may be more extensive.

Fog may also form through the addition of moisture, so that the air becomes so saturated that it is no longer able to hold all of its water vapour. This type of fog occurs in heavy rainfall or through evaporation from a water surface. When the air is very cold the evaporated water may be more than the air can hold, so the excess condenses into fog. The result looks like steam or smoke rising from the sea surface, and because of this it is called arctic sea smoke.

Arctic sea smoke looks like steam or smoke rising from the sea surface.

The cap cloud

It is now time to return to Billy Proctor's question about the cap of fog on Cox Island. This cap of fog is officially called a cap cloud. It forms when air moves up over a mountain, cooling as it rises. The invisible water vapour changes into visible water droplets so that a cloud appears. As the wind blows over the mountain, and moves downward on the far side, the air is warmed, the water droplets evaporate, and the cloud dissipates. With the air continually streaming over the mountain, the process of formation on one side and dissipation on the other continues. The cloud appears to be a single cloud that is stuck in one place, but in reality, it is a process of formation and dissipation. It is ever changing, and ever the same.

Cap clouds don't appear when the air is very dry, as on a bright, sunny summer day, nor in a cold, dry winter outflow. Neither do they form when the air is very moist and saturated, and fog shrouds the entire landscape, nor when a passing weather system brings extensive cloud layers. Cap clouds only form in situations between these two extremes. Cap clouds need movement in the form of strong winds at the mountaintop, and enough - but not too much - moisture to

Cap clouds need movement in the form of strong winds at the mountaintop.

"Since nature is the source of movement and change, and since we are investigating nature, we may not remain ignorant of what movement is; for if we lack this knowledge, we will also remain ignorant of what nature is."

ARISTOTLE

form clouds when the air moves upward over the mountain. Cap clouds say much about the invisible happenings in the air above us. We can all learn about the weather around us if we simply observe the many phenomena of water, warmth, and winds, and allow them to give us clues about their inner workings. Cap clouds have been observed in all parts of the coast and are used as indicators of a variety of weather changes, from the onset of strong northwest winds, to the arrival of fog.

A GLOBAL PICTURE

> From the earth we see the sky
> *Changing before our ever watchful eye*
> *From blue to white and then to black*
> *As rain and wind hits our back.*
> *But when the day is almost done*
> the rainbow marks the return of the sun.

This little poem describes the classic spring-time cycle of the day when all seasons can occur within 24 hours. This is but one weather pattern that we experience along the BC coast. It is a locally driven pattern that develops with the sun heating cold unstable air. Other patterns are more global in nature and require a perspective, not from the earth, but from afar, in order to understand them.

When seen from afar - from cosmic space - the earth appears like a drop of blue water within a sea of black. White clouds, ever changing, float over the surface of blue, with occasional glimpses of brown or green coloured land shining out beneath. The earth, though appearing in isolated glory, is not alone. The moon is its nearest neighbour. The sun is the heart of its life. The planets appear to circle the earth in a weaving dance. The stars form the backdrop for them all. Of all these cosmic bodies, the moon and sun have the greatest impact on water, warmth, and winds.

The impact of the sun on the earth

Light from the sun streams toward the earth. This light, with the energy that it carries, is the main driving force for life on earth. All movements of air and water, in the oceans or in the atmosphere, are stimulated by heat from the sun. Without the sun's energy, water would not be lifted up into the air, nor be changed back from an invisible gas to visible water droplets, or ice crystals that make up the clouds. The sun controls the weather.

The sun appears from earth to be a ball of heat and light, too bright to look at with the naked eye. Only the eagle, within the animal realm, is able to look at it directly. The sun is not a simple yellow ball, but has a range of motions and dynamics that are complex and not fully understood. The earth and the sun, while millions of miles apart, are connected. The earth's atmosphere stretches out into cosmic space, where it meets the extended atmosphere of the sun. Charged particles, called the solar wind, spiral out from the sun, and interact with the magnetic field of the earth to create the magnetosphere. The form of the magnetosphere, contrary to its name, is not spherical at all. Its shape is of a being, with head, shoulders, and a flowing mantle. The mantle stretches out, like a tail, along with the solar wind, as far as the orbit of the moon. This is similar to the tail of a comet, which always extends in a direction away from the sun. When the comet is moving toward the sun its tail stretches out behind it, but when it is moving away from the sun, its tail reaches out ahead of it.

Layers of the atmosphere

When standing on the earth and looking up under a clear blue sky, we cannot tell how high the atmosphere extends. The first exploration of the upper levels of the atmosphere began in the 18th century with the use of hot air balloons that allowed people to be carried above the earth's surface. In these early balloon ascents it was found that the air temperature falls with increasing height above the ground. At the time, this was an amazing revelation. A famous early English meteorologist, Sir Napier Shaw, called it "the most surprising discovery in the whole history of meteorology."

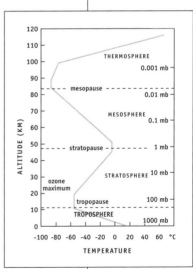

Vertical profile of the atmosphere.

Inside the magnetosphere lies the earth's atmosphere, which like an onion has many layers. The magnetosphere is the magnetic aspect of the atmosphere. The thermosphere is the outer-most physical layer. The next lower layers, the mesosphere, stratosphere, and troposphere, all have the same composition; namely nitrogen (78%), oxygen (21%), with argon and carbon dioxide making up most of the remaining one percent. These percentages are the volumes of each element in a dry atmosphere. But the atmosphere is never completely dry. The amount of water varies considerably in time and space, but on average occupies about 4% of the volume of the troposphere.

The distinguishing feature between these three layers is the way the temperature changes with height above the earth's surface. In the troposphere, the temperature gradually decreases with height. The tropopause marks the upper boundary between the troposphere and the stratosphere. The air temperature generally remains constant, or rises slowly with height through the stratosphere, then falls again through the mesosphere. The stratopause is the boundary between the stratosphere and mesosphere.

Each layer has its own properties and role within the overall structure of the atmosphere. Each layer also has at least one feature that distinguishes it from the others. The aurora occurs in the thermosphere. The mesosphere is the home of noctilucent clouds that are thought to have meteoric dust as the nuclei of the ice particles. They are normally seen just after sunset. The stratosphere contains about 97% of all the ozone in the atmosphere. This ozone is sometimes called high-level ozone, in order to distinguish it from the ozone produced through pollution at the surface. Ozone absorbs ultraviolet rays from the sun, and by so doing limits the amount of ultraviolet rays that reach the surface of the earth. The stratosphere also has its own type of cloud called nacreous, or mother-of-pearl.

Troposphere
The lowest layer of the atmosphere is the realm of life. It is in this layer that we live and breathe. Almost all of the water that exists in the atmosphere is found here, and because of this there is "weather," with its entire array of clouds and precipitation. This layer is called the troposphere. "Tropo" comes from the Greek "tropein" meaning to turn or change, which reflects the significant changing, or transforming, nature of water that occurs within this layer. The ability of water to absorb energy from the sun, and to change from a gas to a liquid, or solid, and back again is the most important driving mechanism of the atmosphere.

The boundary between the water vapour-rich and very active troposphere, and the ozone-rich and relatively quiet stratosphere is the "tropopause." It is not a boundary, like the skin of a balloon, that can be physically observed and felt, but is a very significant threshold none the less. It forms a cap to the upward movement of heat-driven currents that rise from the earth's surface. It is not static and rigid but changes through the day and through the year, rising and falling as the pressure changes. Energy can pass through it in the form of

Almost all of the water that exists in the atmosphere is found in the troposphere and because of this there is "weather."

waves. Breaks, or folds, can also develop within it, allowing the passage of dry, relatively warm stratospheric air, rich in ozone, to flow downward, and water vapour from the troposphere to flow upward. Near the north and south poles, the tropopause is found near eight kilometres above the surface, but rises to about 13 kilometres at the equator.

The hydrosphere and lithosphere

The lowest layers of the earth-atmosphere system are the hydrosphere and the lithosphere. The hydrosphere comprises all the oceans, lakes, rivers, etc., of the earth, and also the water content of the troposphere. The lithosphere is the solid, earthly portion of the planet. The mariner sails between the waters of the ocean and air. The oceans and the lithosphere, like the atmosphere, are also divided into layers based on temperature changes.

The effects of the earth itself on the atmosphere are many and complicated. The main change is brought about because the earth is not uniform; it is made up of continental land masses and bodies of water, of many sizes and shapes. Land heats up and cools down faster than does water. The greater heating over land causes more upward moving air currents. This affects not only the flow of air across the land, but also changes the amount and type of cloud that occurs. Mountains block, or modify the flow of air. Variations of vegetation types influence the heating of the land, and result in modified airflow and cloud types. The oceans, while slower to warm up, retain the heat for much longer and hence act as a source of heat, which they can exchange with the air above them. The oceans are also a vast source of water vapour for the atmosphere. The land generally provides more frictional forces upon the flowing air above it than what occurs over the open ocean. Coastal zones that stand between the oceans and land exhibit a wide variety of effects on the move-ment of both water and air. Details of these are given in the chapter "Weather systems."

The moon and tides

The sun, of all the cosmic bodies, has the strongest role to play in the move-ments on earth. The moon is next in line, with its notable role in the formation of ocean tides. Mariners have lived with the rhythms of the tides ever since the first person set sail on the water. The tides are as much a part of the life of a mariner as are the winds that blow over the water. The mariner sails in that realm between two moving fluids, the air above, and the water below. One

The highest recorded ascent of an open hot air balloon occurred in 1901, when two German scientists rose to 10.5 km. They were able to record a temperature reading of -32° near this height, moments before they drifted into unconsciousness.

difference between these two moving fluids is that one is readily visible for all to see, and the other is not.

"Once again with the tide she slips her lines
Turns her head and comes awake."
THE FIRST LINES OF THE SONG *BLUENOSE* BY STAN ROGERS

The earth and moon rotate around their common centre of mass, which is found, not at the centre of the earth, but at about 1700 km beneath the surface of the earth. The gravitational pulls of each on the other causes a bulge of water to extend out from the earth's surface toward the moon and a second bulge of water to extend out on the opposite side away from the moon. A way to picture this is to think of the first bulge as water being pulled more strongly towards the moon than is the earth, and the second bulge resulting from the earth being more strongly pulled than the water. The earth then rotates under these two bulges.

The two bulges of water can be seen as two crests of a wave that circle the earth. Between these two crests the sea level falls with the approach of the trough of the wave and rises with the approach of the tidal wave crest. The tidal waves move around the earth, following the movement of the moon.

Tidal wave motion as seen off the BC coast.

> It should be kept in mind that a tsunami, a wave created by earthquakes and land slumps, is incorrectly called a tidal wave, it is not connected with tides at all.

The tidal wave is a progressive wave, to use the terminology described earlier. The form of the wave moves at speeds near 400 knots, but the water, fortunately, does not move forward with the wave. The wave is simply a form that is created in the water. The water of the ocean rises and falls with the passage of the form.

Amphidromic points

If the earth had no continental land mass, the tides would be as simple as just described, but because the oceans are confined to separate basins the tides are much more complicated. What is found is that the tidal wave moves around a single point within a basin. This point, called the amphidromic point, sees no rising or falling of the tides. The amphidromic point closest to the BC coast is just north of Hawaii. Since, in the northern hemisphere, the wave rotates counterclockwise around the amphidromic points, the tidal wave moves northward along the coast. It takes about 12 hours for a complete rotation of the wave. Lines that mark the passage of one phase of the tidal wave, say the highest point of the wave, or the high tide, are called cophase, or cotidal lines. These lines, one for each hour of the cycle, are represented approximately on the map. They are not uniformly spaced since the speed of the wave is affected by water depth.

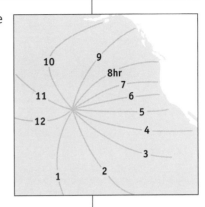

The hourly movements of the tides around the amphidromic point north of Hawaii.

Flood and ebb tides

As the crest of the tidal wave approaches, the water rises and runs downhill, so to speak, away from the crest. The rising water is called the "flood tide" and the horizontal movement of water is the tidal current or stream. With the passage of the tidal wave crest there is a short period of quiet or slack water, then the water begins to stream toward the approaching trough of the wave. The falling water level is called the "ebb tide." The tidal current now flows in the opposite direction.

The horizontal movements of water are strongly affected by the shape of the coastline. The currents are steered by the shape of the coastline, and are sped up when forced through narrow channels or over shallower bottoms. Friction near the edge of the flowing currents also causes eddies to form. Some currents responding to the ebbing tide may still be exiting from some long channels when the currents from the next flooding tide are met. Since the two water streams have followed different paths in their six-hour (or more) history, they may have developed slightly different water temperatures. Because of this, the two water streams may not simply merge when they encounter one another but will form a boundary between them. Along this boundary, eddies form, just as they do near the hard boundary at the sides of the channel.

Tidal streams follow the same paths each day, but since the height of the tide changes from one day to the next the exact pattern of the flow varies. The difference between high and low water is called the tidal range. With a large tidal range the strength of the tidal currents will be greater, as will the strength of all local modifications to the flow. This means that the eddies that form in some locations will be much stronger and much more dangerous. Some eddies that form because of specific topographical conditions are so predictable that

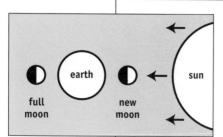

SPRING TIDE

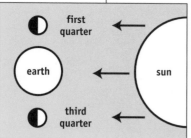

NEAP TIDE

they are plotted on the Canadian Hydrographic Service charts. In small inlets and bays the tide tends to just oscillate back and forth within the inlet. The height of the tide, however, is usually somewhat larger at the inner end of the bay or inlet.

The cycle of the tides reaches its highest point when both the sun and moon lie in a straight line through the earth. These higher tides, called "spring tides" occur at new and full moon and are not connected with the spring season. When the sun and moon are at right angles to each other, at the quarter moon, the result is a "neap tide."

There are three major types of tides: diurnal tides that have one high and one low per day, semi-diurnal tides that have two equal highs and lows each day, and mixed tides that have two unequal highs and lows each day. Within the Pacific Ocean, due to the complex interplay of tides around the amphidromic points, all three types of tides can be found.

The actual height of the tides is affected by the atmospheric pressure. If the pressure is low there is less air above to push down on the water, and the tides will be higher than predicted, but if the pressure is high there is more air pushing down from above and the tides are lower. The height of the tides is most evident at the dock where mariners have observed them to be as much as three feet higher or lower than predicted.

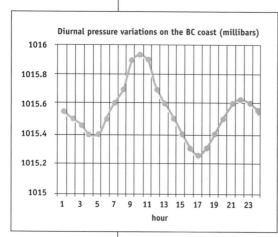

Diurnal pressure variations on the BC coast (millibars)

Atmospheric tides

The atmosphere also has its tide, which, unlike ocean tides, is most strongly connected with the sun. Ocean tides occur approximately 50 minutes later each day, since the moon rises later each day by that amount. Atmospheric tides, on the other hand, occur at set times every day, in accord with the sun's daily rhythm. The cause of the atmospheric tide is still not known for certain. The atmospheric pressure is lowest near 0400 hours, and again at 1600 hours, with maximum pressures near 1000 and 2200 hours. The times of lowest pressure occur near the times of the rising and setting of the sun - the out-breathing and in-breathing of the earth. The atmospheric tide has its greatest amplitude and is most regular at the equator but is barely observable in the mid-latitudes, where the passage of high and low pressure systems brings strong pressure changes. The double rhythm of maximum and minimum pressure is similar to the double rhythm of semi-diurnal ocean tides.

Global movements of air

The movements of the oceans of water and air are largely controlled by the sun. This is particularly true for large scale motions, for smaller scale motions can be influenced by factors other than solar heating. Global scale movements within the atmosphere can be seen in satellite pictures that cover the entire earth. This is possible because clouds are the visible form of invisible processes, or movements.

In 1735, an English meteorologist named George Hadley first presented his idea that the strong heating of the sun over the equator, and the cold temperatures at the poles, must create a circulation between them. The idea was that air rises upwards and moves toward the pole, with a return circulation taking place at the surface, from the pole to the equator. This theory might have arisen from the thought that the equator, even with daily strong heating from the sun, doesn't continue to get hotter and hotter, but remains more or less the same temperature throughout the year, and from year to year. Likewise, the poles don't continue to get colder. So a mechanism must exist that redistributes the heat from areas of excess, to where it is less. It was a good theory, which, as it turned out, wasn't quite correct.

Within the fluid motions of the atmosphere there are wave motions of all dimensions, from ones that encircle the globe to the tiniest eddies seen in the smoke from a candle. These larger waves are called "global" scale phenomena and can extend over thousands of kilometres, with periods of oscillation of days or weeks. The smallest of the wave motions are called "micro" scale and extend over fractions of metres, with periods less than a second. The major high and low pressure systems, which cause our weather, fall between these two scales, and are called "synoptic" scale features. Many of the interesting local phenomena of wind and weather are smaller scale than the synoptic, and are called "meso," or "local" scale. They include the features that arise from fluid-type interactions with topography. All of the waves interact and send their effects up and down the scales of motion.

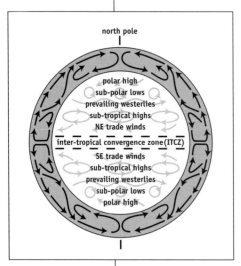

Global wind circulation cells.

The rotation of the earth on its axis, and the existence of continental land masses modify this simple picture. The more correct pattern, according to the latest information, does not have one circulation cell, but three. The diagram shows the resultant movements across the face of the earth as well as the vertically rotating cells that develop between the earth and the tropopause. The BC coast lies within the belt of prevailing westerlies, but is strongly influenced by the strength and movement of the subtropical high to the south and the subpolar low to the north. The polar front that separates the polar easterlies from the prevailing westerlies is not a rigid boundary but moves north and south with changes to the strength and position of the westerlies.

All objects that move across the face of the earth, whether they are planes, water or air, appear deflected toward the right in the northern hemisphere, and to the left in the southern hemisphere, because the earth is rotating under them. When viewed from space an object moving in a straight line does just that. But when viewed from the perspective of our moving earth the same motion is not seen as a straight line but as a curve. It appears that there is some force that deflects it from its path. This force was given the name, Coriolis, after Gaspard-Gustave de Coriolis, a French mathematician, who wrote a scientific paper published in 1835 describing movements within a moving frame of reference. While there is no actual force that causes the moving object to turn in direction, the change in direction is totally real - from our earth-bound perspective.

The southeast trade winds converge with the northeast trade winds at what is called the inter-tropical convergence zone, which is frequently shortened to ITCZ. The ITCZ might appear to be so far from the BC coast that it wouldn't have any impact, but recent years have shown this to be untrue, for we have become aware that El Niño and La Niña can influence the weather over the entire Pacific, if not the entire globe. The first hint that weather changes in the tropics affect other parts of the globe came in the late nineteenth and early twentieth century, when studies were done on pressure changes between Australia and Argentina. A few years later, Gilbert Walker, a British mathematician, noted that when pressures rise in the India-Australia area, they usually fall in South America. He called this the "Southern Oscillation," and later went on to theorize that these changes were not just a tropical affair, but that weather was a global phenomenon.

The basic pattern of weather, within the stream of westerlies, can be visualized as two pillars. One, in which air from the heights warms as it moves down to the surface of the earth, represents the high. The other, the low, has air rising from below, up into the heights. It cools as it moves upward. Between these two forms that appear, disappear, and appear again, the entire range of weather develops: sun, clouds, rain, rainbows and sun again. The two spiralling forms are invisible, but ever-present. They stand as if behind a veil - a veil of chaos. They stand at the doorway between us on earth, and the cosmic rhythms of the universe.

The circulation patterns of the ocean reflect the global scale atmospheric motions.

Global ocean movements

The upper layers of the ocean move, primarily, due to the winds that blow over them, and are steered by Coriolis forces. As a result, the circulation patterns of the ocean reflect the global scale atmospheric motions. The main difference between the atmosphere and the ocean is that the oceans are limited to ocean basins, while the atmosphere is not. This results in large circulations, gyres, developing in each ocean basin.

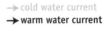

Over the Pacific Ocean the strong belt of westerlies in the atmosphere creates the North Pacific Current. This current turns southward off California, in the strong northwest winds, and enters the eastward flowing return loop of the North equatorial current that is driven by the northeast trade winds. The Alaskan gyre results from the persistent presence of low pressure systems in the Gulf of Alaska, giving easterly winds to the far northern regions.

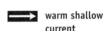
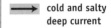

The deep ocean circulations are driven, however, not by winds, but by differences in density of the water. Density changes are caused by changes in the temperature and salinity of the water. These two factors are called "thermohaline," with "thermo" meaning temperature, and "haline," salt. The circulation is a complex loop that moves as a cold current in the lower realms of the ocean, from the north Atlantic to the north Pacific, then rises and travels back toward the Atlantic as a warmer, near-surface current. The entire cycle takes about 1000 years.

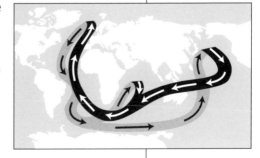

Sea surface temperatures

Water has a great capacity to store and move heat. The heat storing capacity of the ocean plays a major role in the energy exchange of the entire ocean-atmosphere system. The heat required to warm the top three metres of the ocean by one Celsius degree, is enough to warm the entire atmosphere by the same amount. The oceans are therefore able to store the summer heat and to slowly release it during the following winter, thereby protecting coastal areas from large extremes in temperature. The oceans are also able, through the global circulations, to transport heat from equatorial regions toward the poles. The significance of the ocean temperatures has become more widely known through recent studies of the El Niño/La Niña phenomenon, which show that water temperature changes have a major impact on global weather patterns.

Ocean salinity

The saltiness of the ocean is rather interesting. It has often been said that the saltiness of the oceans results from the minerals carried into the oceans from the world's rivers. But river water has only a small amount of salt, which is primarily calcium and bicarbonate ions, while seawater salts are largely sodium and chloride. The latest theory is that the saltiness comes from out-gassing of minerals from vents, rifts, and volcanoes on the ocean floor. The salt content of the oceans is almost uniform throughout the world at about 35 parts of salt per one thousand parts of water (written 35‰). It is rarely less than 33‰ and seldom more than 38‰. Salinities are much lower in coastal waters, near the mouths of large rivers, and in the polar seas, where there is ice-melt.

The salt content of the ocean is higher than it is in the human body. While the average ocean salt content is around 35 ‰, the human blood has a salt content near 9 ‰. This is why salt water does not quench thirst. Water moves through body tissues, from areas of less saltiness to where the saltiness is higher. Hence, by drinking salt water, water from the body tissues would leave the tissues and move into the salt water, leaving the body more dehydrated than it was before.

THE CYCLE OF THE YEAR

Weather is a beautifully complex subject. It borders on the realm of chaos. But it is only at the edge of chaos, for within the seeming infinite variety of weather changes that occur, there are patterns that can be recognized. We can say, for instance, that on our coast summer is warmer and drier than winter and has less wind. We know that the weather in any month of this year will be similar, in general terms, to that experienced last year or to that which will be experienced next year. These repeating patterns, or rhythms, are primarily the result of movements of the earth, sun, and moon, and of the changes on the earth that these movements bring about.

Weather, like music, is made of many tones and many rhythms that interweave to create the final work. The main background rhythm that affects the daily progression of weather systems onto the coast is the rhythm of the seasons. With this view, the year is not seen as a linear event, with one day following after the other, as pages are turned in a calendar. It is more of a circle, or a song without end, which rotates endlessly, from summer through autumn, winter to spring, and back again to summer. It is a beautiful picture of completeness, of a whole. Many stories, legends, and pictures of the First Nations on our coast express the wonder and fullness of this complete, never-ending cycle.

The daily rhythm of the sun rising in the morning and setting each evening is basic to all life on earth. This daily pattern is repeated in the cycle of the year as the sun rises higher in the sky in spring, reaching its peak in late June, then falls again through the autumn until late December. A cycle of a much greater magnitude, called the platonic year, lasts for approximately 25,920 years. This cycle is caused by a wobble in the rotation of the earth on its axis. The earth's axis presently points toward the "pole star" at the end of the constellation Ursa Major (the Big Dipper). But over the millennia the earth's axis rotates completely around the celestial sphere. This rhythm was discovered when early astronomers noted that the position of the sun at the spring equinox moved slightly backward through the zodiac each year. It takes 25,920 years for the axis to return to its starting place. This movement, sometimes called the "precession of the equinox," forms, perhaps, the outer boundary to the rhythms that affect the earth. Between the daily cycle and the platonic year, all other rhythms - whether seen or unseen - sound their part and combine to produce the variety of weather that we experience every day of the year.

The daily rhythm of the sun rising in the morning and setting each evening is basic to all life on earth. This daily pattern is repeated in the cycle of the year as the sun rises higher in the sky in spring, then falls again through the autumn until late December.

Cycles of rain and wind

Soon after beginning work on this book I started to look at the cycle of the year, and how it showed itself in the climate records of various stations on the coast. One of my first studies was to look at the record for winds at Herbert Island, in Queen Charlotte Strait. Instead of looking at monthly mean values, which is most commonly done, I looked at weekly means. Graphs of monthly means give the general picture of the year, but show little that a coastal resident doesn't already know. The attached graph of Egg Island, for example, is based on monthly averages and shows that winter is windier than summer. The graph for the winds at Herbert Island using weekly averages, however, shows a variety of features that are interesting, and call out for an explanation.

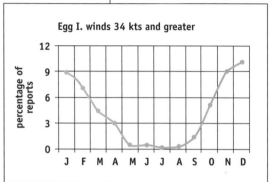

MONTHLY WINDS Egg Island where winds in winter are windier than summer.

The values on the bottom of the graph are for the first week of each month. The data for these graphs came from the entire record of information of each station. The records for Egg and Herbert islands only go back to 1985, while two other stations, Bella Coola and Quatsino have records dating back to 1896. In the records of precipitation (which is mainly rain, for the amount of snowfall on the coast is quite low), the weekly periods have days with greater or lesser amounts of rain.

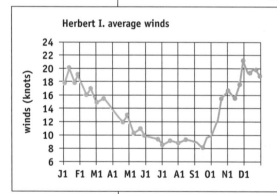

WEEKLY WINDS Herbert Island winds show a variety of features that are interesting and call out for explanation.

Over fifteen coastal stations were studied, and they all show similar pauses, or peaks, for both rainfall and wind strength - at almost the same times of year. The similarity was most dramatic from July through December. One would think that over this long period of record, and this many stations, random variations of wind and rain would be averaged out. Two questions come to mind. Why are the peaks and troughs at these specific times, and what causes them? It should be noted that these changes in frequency of winds and rainfall are not great, and in many cases might not be noticed. But the fact that they occur at all coastal stations, at the same time, suggests that there are specific rhythms in our weather that are hidden behind the veil of apparent chaos of our daily weather.

In the search for answers to these questions many people were asked in the hopes that someone would be able to suggest something that is changing at these times of the year, which might be the reason for the pauses and peaks. A few people made suggestions, but no one gave definitive answers. The best suggestion came from a fellow forecaster in Halifax, George Parks, who thought that the pause in frequency of gales in mid-November could be related to the source of the storms. Late summer, until

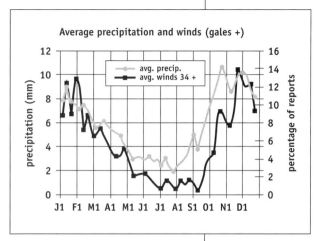

early November, is a time for typhoons to develop. Typhoon is the name for a hurricane on the west side of the International Date Line. Many of these typhoons form off the Philippines and die as they cross the colder waters of the north Pacific. But the moisture of these systems continues moving eastward, and sometimes helps to redevelop storms as they approach the BC coast. After this period of typhoons has passed, the storms that arrive on the coast are just normal mid-latitude storms and have a different origin of their moisture. The idea is that the pause seen on the graphs represents the shift between the two cycles of tropical storms and mid-latitude storms. This might explain the dip in mid-November, but doesn't explain the others.

Coastal stations show similar pauses, or peaks, for both rainfall and wind strength.

The search for explanations

In the search for other explanations of the various peaks and pauses, temperature differences between air and water, and pressure differences from north to south were studied. The temperature of the world's oceans and land masses is increased as the sun rises higher in the sky, and cools as the sun-angle lowers. The land, however, rises in temperature faster than the oceans, and likewise, cools more quickly. The atmosphere near the earth's surface tends to conform to the temperature of the water, or land, beneath it. As a result, the air over the land is warmer than the air over the water through the spring and summer months, and is cooler than the water temperature in autumn and winter. These temperature differences result in sea-breeze type inflow winds in the warm, summer half of the year, and outflow winds in the cooler months.

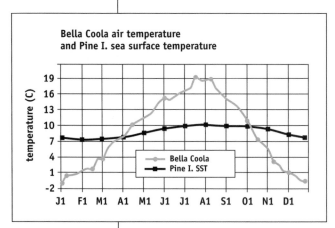

Bella Coola air temperature and Pine I. sea surface temperature

The graph for air temperatures at Bella Coola, and water temperatures at Pine Island shows that the air becomes warmer (on average) than the water in March, and becomes colder than the water in late September and early October. As a result, westerly inflow winds prevail from April through September, and easterly, outflow winds from October through March. This pattern is confirmed by the shift of the dominant winds at two coastal stations, Cathedral Point and Nanakwa Shoal Buoy, in Douglas Channel.

North to south pressure differences

As the sun moves northward in the spring, the height of the tropopause rises, and the pressure increases. The time of the year when the pressure is highest is not at the solstice at the end of June, but in late July. Similarly, the time of the lowest pressure is not at the winter solstice but during the first week of December. While this timing of pressure changes is the same in all parts of the coast, the actual pressure is higher in the south compared to the north. The northern areas are closer to the lows that normally reside over the Gulf of Alaska, and the southern stations are closer to the sub-tropical high. As a result, the pressure in the north is generally lower than places farther south. The only time of the year when the average pressure in the north is greater than in the south is the period from mid-July to mid-August. This corresponds to the premium boating period on the coast.

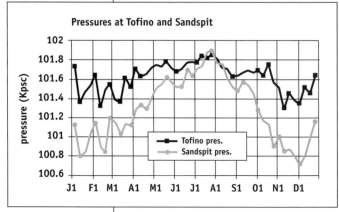

Pressures at Tofino and Sandspit

In order to study the north to south pressure differences, average weekly pressures at two southern stations, Vancouver and Tofino, were compared with the average pressure values at Prince Rupert and Sandspit. The pressure values from these four stations effectively created a pressure-slope for the coast.

The earlier Environment Canada publication, *The Wind Came All Ways,* introduced the concept of the pressure-slope. The pressure-slope simplified and summarized the many changes of wind patterns that can occur in a topographically rich region, such as the Georgia Basin. It was primarily an educational tool. The pressure-slope plane is a representation of the pressure surface between a ridge and trough. The plane can be rotated in any direction, and can be at any angle from the horizontal. The winds flow down the slope just as water flows downhill. Winds blow from high pressure to low pressure. The steeper the angle, the greater the pressure-slope gradient and the potential for stronger winds.

When the pressure is higher in the south, the plane slopes downward from south to north. This is called a southerly pressure-slope. During the course of the year this pressure-slope rises and falls in value, and amazingly, when graphed it almost exactly mimics the pattern of weekly precipitation averages, especially during the period from July through December.

When there is a pause in the precipitation, the pressure difference from south to north is not as great. This reflects the fact that most rainfall occurs with southeast winds ahead of fronts. And since the lows associated with the fronts move into the Gulf of Alaska, the pressure is lower in the north. So when there is even a small change in the pressure-slope (remembering that these are averages), then the amount of precipitation changes. The change in pressure-slope of the coast could almost be

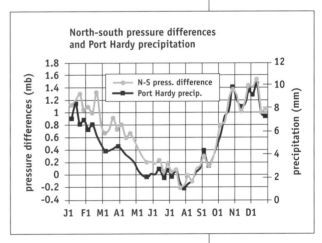

a substitute for the yearly changes in precipitation. The similarity between the pressure differences and the winds could also be seen to result from the fact that the winds tend to be strongest ahead of the fronts (i.e. when the pressure is highest to the south), and are less after the fronts have passed (when the pressure is not quite as low in the north).

North-south pressure differences compared with Port Hardy precipitation.

A year in review

The results from these studies can be summarized in a descriptive overview of the year. Through the summer the winds are light, the temperatures are at their warmest values of the year, and on average, the amount of rainfall reaches its lowest point at the end of July. This is summer at its best. From this point through the remainder of the summer there are occasional showers that tend to increase in intensity, if not in frequency, until early September. Then toward mid-September there is a pause, the showers decrease, the sun shines brightly and the winds remain light. It is a brilliant time of the year.

As the autumn equinox approaches, conditions on the coast normally begin their most dramatic change. The first storm of the season usually arrives at this time, along with overcast skies and steady rain. The temperatures of both the air and ocean begin to fall. Occasionally a series of two or three storms follow one after the other, which may be the last of the ex-typhoons, then again there is a pause. This time the pause is brief, and does not return to the glory of summer as it does in mid-September. Then progressively through October and into early November, the storms become stronger and more frequent. A peak in both rainfall and the strength of winds takes place in late October, or early November. In mid-November there is another pause. This time it is likely due to the building of a ridge of high pressure over the interior, and the first hint of outflow winds. The frequency of gales and the rainfall amounts are both reduced. Then the frequency of lows approaching the coast increases again, and reaches its yearly high in late November, or early December. Then there is another pause, this time of longer duration, and of greater impact. The mood of the year has definitely changed, autumn is over; winter has begun.

Through the latter part of December, the upper flow often develops a blocking pattern, with a strong ridge of high pressure over the BC interior. The temperatures, both on the coast and across the interior of the province drop to their lowest values. Arctic air becomes fully established over the interior and spills out at times onto the coast. In January and February there is a see-saw oscillation between weather systems approaching from the west, and outflow winds spreading to the coast from the east. The frequency of gales and precipitation amounts drop with outflow events, and rise with the approach of offshore storms. While the frequency of both winds and precipitation (at this time of year it could also include snow) is less than in early December, it

Approximately 70% of the earth's surface is covered with water. Most of this water, over 97%, in fact, is found within the oceans of the world. During a torrential downpour we may be overwhelmed by the amount of water falling from the sky, but on average, the atmosphere only has about one thousandth of one percent (.001%) of the water found on earth.

takes an even greater drop at the end of February, or in early March. This marks the beginning of spring, which normally sees rapid changes from sun, to cloud and rain, and back to sun again, but overall has a marked decrease in rainfall and wind strength. The frequency of gales over most of the coast drops off to near zero by early summer, but the rainfall amounts don't fall to their lowest values until the end of July. The cycle of the year is now completed.

The four seasons

The turning points of the year can be determined from the cycles shown in the previous graphs. If the lowest point of the precipitation cycle in late July marks the halfway point of the season, then summer includes the months of June, July, and August. Autumn begins with the peak in precipitation in early September, and continues until the peak in late November or early December. Winter begins when the steady onslaught of weather systems slows dramatically in mid-December, and continues through several periods of outflow events until the end of February. Spring begins with the drop in precipitation in late February or early March, and continues through May. It is easiest to use whole calendar months for each season, but the graphs suggest that the seasons actually begin in the second week of the month, not at the very beginning of the month. These seasonal definitions beginning mid-month, which are based on climate studies, are within a few days of the traditional definitions.

The four winds

The four seasons can also be connected to certain winds. The seasonal winds are not necessarily the dominant ones of each season, but provide the overriding signature, or tone, of that season. Autumn and winter both lie in the period of easterly winds, while spring and summer are in the time of westerlies. The period from late July to early December occurs when the pressure-slope is becoming more and more strongly southerly. The other half of the year has a trend of a decreasing southerly pressure-slope. From these changes the signature wind of autumn is southeast; winter is northeast, and spring is southwest. Summer starts out northwest, but changes to southwest partway through.

The four seasons can be connected to certain winds. The seasonal winds are not necessarily the dominant ones of each season, but provide the overriding signature, or tone, of that season.

AUTUMN	September, October and November	SOUTHEAST
WINTER	December, January and February	NORTHEAST
SPRING	March, April and May	SOUTHWEST
SUMMER	June, July and August	NORTHWEST

In most years, each season appears to have three parts. The first part reflects the season that has just passed, the last hints of the season to come, and the middle period bears what could be called the "true" season. The pauses between each part have been called "singularities" in the climate records. They could also be called the "meteorological turning points" of the year. The fact that they happen at specific times of the year, for almost all coastal stations, implies that a certain collection of rhythms are involved. While the average timing of these singularities seem to be quite well fixed on the calendar, the actual time of their occurrence from year to year is not as fixed.

The lemniscate rhythm of the year

The year can be viewed in a number of ways. The simple progression from one day to the next is a linear perspective, which sees the year pass with the daily turn of the calendar. First Nations people tend to view the year as a circle, with the seasons rolling by one after the other, with no beginning, and no end. This endless cycle can also be represented by a lemniscate, which has the advantage of also reflecting the shift from inward to outward aspects, in a breathing type of rhythm. All nature expresses, in one way or another, a breathing rhythm. The plants spring into life and begin to grow. As summer proceeds, the growth slows and the work of the year is compressed into the fruit or seed.

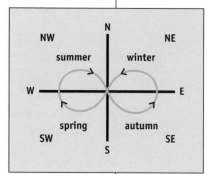

The outward growth is turned inward into the seed. This inwardness remains throughout the autumn and winter before it blossoms forth again in spring. Humanity also goes through a similar cycle, though it is masked by the much greater range of activities that we have, compared to a plant. But this inward and outward breathing can still be experienced as a sort of waking up to the world around us in spring, and in greater activity in the outside world of nature in summer. For many people there is a noticeable shift from the hectic outward activities of summer, to the more inward times of autumn and winter.

Dancing water

Before going on to seek a greater understanding of the rhythms reflected in the pressure-slope cycle of the year, I would like to add a personal story. During a trip that I made to the north coast to talk to people about their weather experiences, I encountered a young professional fishing couple who described something I had never heard of before. They said that one day they were out on the water and the pressure was falling rapidly, but before the winds rose, the water began to dance. Droplets were bouncing up off the water. It only lasted a couple of minutes before the winds gave a couple of stronger puffs, then rose quickly to about 60 knots. I found this very interesting but did not know how to explain it. A few days later, when visiting Barkerville as a tourist, I saw what I think is the same phenomenon. There was a display of two ancient Chinese sounding bowls. These bronze bowls had handles on either side of the rim, and were partially filled with water. By rhythmically rubbing the handles, the water began to dance, with water droplets jumping up off the surface. I tucked these two coincidental events away, for I was not sure what to do with them. Ideas about these phenomena will be given later.

"If we wish to achieve a contemplation of nature that is somewhat alive, we must see that we remain as mobile and plastic as the example nature provides us."

J.W. von GOETHE

Weather is a process that involves a continual interweaving of many elements, on many different scales. With only slight changes to any one of the elements, the weather that we experience may differ dramatically. The task of the weather forecaster is to look at the interweaving of as many weather elements as possible and create a "best guess" as to how the combined result will unfold during the next few hours or days. Since the potential combinations of interactions are so complex, computer programs are used to do much of this work. Over the years these computer programs have become more and more sophisticated, and include finer and finer details of the different interactions, but still they are not perfect. Perhaps weather forecasting will never be perfect, for the number of variables and possible interweavings is so great. Edward N. Lorenz, who gave a talk in 1972 titled, "Does the flap of a butterfly's wings in Brazil set off a tornado in Texas?", came to his conclusion that a perfect forecast is impossible because weather is chaotic.

Overlapping of cycles

Some meteorologists continue to search for finer and finer scales of interactions of weather variables, while others look at atmosphere-ocean cycles that take place over vast areas, over decades or centuries of time. Many of these longer term changes, or oscillations, are now frequently talked about in the media, as well as in scientific circles. The El Niño and La Niña events are perhaps best known, but others such as the Pacific Decadal Oscillation (PDO) are less well known.

A look at ocean tides may throw light on the combining of different cycles. Anyone who has used tide tables regularly will be aware that the pattern of high and low tides repeat about 50 minutes later each day. They will have also noticed that the biggest tides occur near the solstices, in June and December. These are but two of the many variations of the daily tidal pattern. It takes the passage of almost 19 years before the tidal pattern comes close to repeating itself. The reason for these many variations is that the rhythms of the sun and moon, which drive the tides, are so very complex. Scientists have found that they can break any tidal pattern down into a combination of simple waves, called sine waves. Each sine wave has a slightly different period, height, and phase. The mathematical procedure to do this is called harmonic analysis. From this kind of study a total of 390 different cycles, or tide components, have been identified.

The state of the sea, with its short period chop and long swells, can be broken down into individual wave forms.

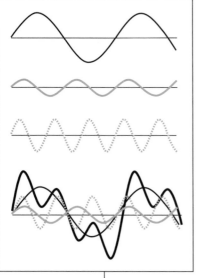

The complex collection of waves on the ocean can be viewed in a similar fashion. The state of the sea, with its short period chop, and long swells, can be broken down into individual wave forms. The accompanying diagram shows three different waves and how they merge into one more complicated wave pattern. In a completely different realm, music can also be analyzed in the same way, to separate the different frequencies of sound that occur. Sound is a wave phenomenon just like the waves on the ocean, and the tides of the world.

Weather cycles

Weather, as a wave phenomenon, can also be viewed as the result of the combination of different waves, or rhythms. The strongest rhythm, the yearly path around the sun, gives the pattern of the seasons. The daily rhythm is another cycle, which is seen most strongly during the summer when passing weather systems don't overshadow it. Other rhythms of longer periods involve the interplay between the rhythms of the oceans and air, such as the oscillations known as El Niño and La Niña. The duration of these cycles is about 6 to 18 months. An El Niño cycle generally occurs once every 2 to 7 years. Another rhythm, which has a similar pattern and effect as El Niño and La Niña, but lasts much longer, is called the Pacific Decadal Oscillation (PDO) and involves periods of warm or cold waters, each lasting 20 to 30 years. All of these oscillations are like waves, that combine and interact, producing different results with each new combination. The final result is our weather.

Water and sound

Since both weather and music are wave phenomena, all of the descriptions that apply to sound waves, such as amplitude, interference, and reflection, have their exact counterpart in the motions of ocean waves and in the waves of weather. Weather and music both result from waves within air. Weather, however, has water, and music has sound.

The idea of weather being related to sound raises a number of interesting thoughts. An eighteenth century scientist, Ernest Chladni, born in 1756, found that by moving a violin bow over a flat plate covered with sand, various patterns and shapes could be created. These forms are now called Chladni figures. He demonstrated that physical form was related to sound. Then there are the legends that the Navajo Indians, who were famous for their sand paintings, told about the time when their shamans produced pictures in the sand by merely speaking to it. And finally in a similar perspective, there is the biblical story in which Jesus, caught in a sudden storm on the lake of Galilee, spoke to the wind and to the water, and there was calm. All this suggests that movement of air, whether it is sound (music or words) or wind, is related to form. Forms that appear in the atmosphere, oceans, and on earth are affected, if not caused, by certain wave motions. Light is also a wave phenomenon that manifests in specific forms, namely colours.

Ernest Chladni, born in 1756, found that by moving a violin bow over a flat plate covered with sand, various patterns and shapes were created.

33

Returning now to the phenomenon of the dancing waters. I do not have an exact explanation but it seems that the water in the Chinese bowl was set in motion by a specific vibration of the bowl - by a specific sounding rhythm. The ocean waters, likewise, were likely set into motion through a specific vibration of the water, or the air above it. How this vibration was created is unknown to me, but may well be related to the fact that the pressure was falling rapidly, which means that the atmosphere was going through a dramatic shift of structure. It might also be connected with some kind of resonance, or reflection between that body of water and the mountainous surroundings. However it is viewed, it seems that the answer may be found through an understanding of the sounding of rhythms.

Weather is an amazing phenomenon, one that cannot be fully understood by any single person, nor explained by any one book. A complete picture of all the forces that are at play within the atmosphere remains just beyond our sight - just behind the veil of chaos. We can only open our eyes to the many expressions of weather, and let them speak to us.

Could we not explain all visible form, from a crystal up to man, as being brought about through movement that sounded, and then stopped.

Sound seems to be nothing but broken movement, in the sense that colour is broken light. NOVALIS FRAGMENTS

weather systems

HIGHS, LOWS, FRONTS, AND RIDGES

COASTAL EFFECTS

> Still waters run deep and are quiet.
> *Moving waters are seen and enliven.*

The movement of fluids, both water and air, was looked at in general terms in the previous chapter. Here the focus will be on what changes take place when a moving fluid encounters obstacles in its path. The next two chapters focus even more on the specific effects that the BC coast, with its islands, mountain ranges, and inlets has on the local flow of moving water and air. Since there is such a strong similarity between moving waters and moving air they will be considered together. A third example, that of sound, could be added, for its movements are similar, but this is left to the reader to consider.

Friction

Moving water and air are not able to penetrate into a hard physical object so are deflected in one way or another by it. When water and air pass over an object, the speed of motion is slowed by friction. The friction effect varies with the type of surface that is encountered. A smooth surface causes less friction than a rough, irregular surface. Air moving over water experiences less friction than air moving over land. The type of landforms also makes a difference. Tree cover causes more frictional effects than bare fields.

When water and air pass over an object, the speed of motion is slowed by friction.

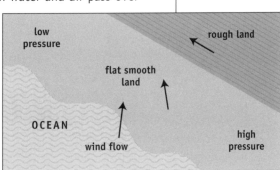

But friction does more than slow the movement of a fluid; it also changes its direction. Air moving from water onto land is backed (i.e. rotated counter-clockwise) from the direction that it was when moving over water. The air turns toward lower pressure, which according to Buys-Ballot's law is on your left when the winds are at your back. Winds blow from higher to lower pressure.

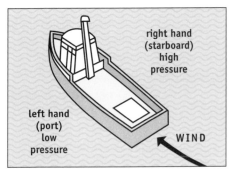

Buys-Ballot's Law - with the wind at your back, low pressure is to your left.

> Slow-moving fluids, be they air or water, gently conform to the shape of the topography they move past. Faster moving fluids, on the other hand, interact with the topography and produce a variety of significant changes.

This turning of the winds by the land creates an area of convergence between the backed winds over the land with the winds over the water. This convergence

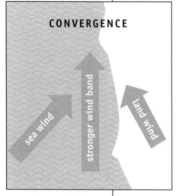

CONVERGENCE

sea wind

stronger wind band

land wind

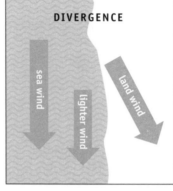

DIVERGENCE

sea wind

lighter wind

land wind

can cause the winds to increase in speed by as much as 25-50%. The location of this band of strong winds varies somewhat depending on the actual strength and direction of winds, but generally lies within a few miles of shore. Water moving along a sloping beach will also generate a band of faster moving water because of convergence with the non-slowed water offshore. When the flow has the land on the left the slower winds over the land diverge from the stronger winds over the sea to create an area of somewhat lighter winds offshore.

Stronger winds are created with convergence and weaker winds with divergence.

Steering and enhancing

Moving fluids, not being able to go through solid objects, are forced to flow along the orientation of the coastline. This is called "steering" or "channelling." If the water or air is not only steered by the topography but also forced through a narrow gap, then it is strengthened through "venturi" effects. This

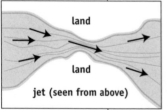

land

land

jet (seen from above)

is called "funnelling." Winds that are funnelled are called gap winds. Water that is funnelled forms a strong current, or jet. The plume of stronger flowing water or air tends to be strongest near the centre of the passageway and weakest near the edge. Keep in mind though, that fluids move like waves so there may be a certain amount of wave-like oscillations of the plume. This plume normally extends a short distance beyond the opening of the passageway before dissipating and being turned in the direction of the prevailing flow outside the gap. The stronger the flow in the gap, the greater the distance that it extends outside the gap.

Moving fluids increase in speed through topographical constrictions.

Corner effects

"Corner effects" are caused by funnelling between an obstacle such as a headland or peninsula, and the main flow of wind or water. When a tidal current, or flow of winds, approaches a peninsula, it is partially blocked along one side and is forced to go around the obstacle. The flow that is seaward of the peninsula acts as a soft boundary that prevents the deflected stream from moving farther out. A band of stronger winds develops between these two parts of the flow. Coastal convergence can also add to this strengthening. The band of stronger flow will extend some distance beyond the peninsula. Eddies form to the lee of the peninsula; these may appear either as small vortices in the water, or as gusts from different directions in the invisible air.

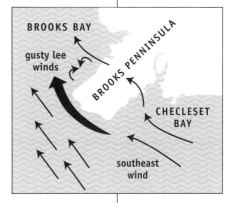

"Corner effects" are caused by funnelling between an obstacle and the main flow of wind or water.

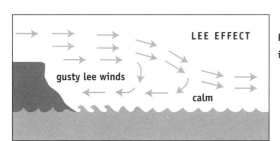

LEE EFFECT

Eddies form to the lee of islands and peninsulas.

←

The temperature profile of water and the stability of air both have an impact on the way they respond to physical boundaries. With unstable air the flow around the outside of the headland is reduced as some air is able to flow up over the peninsula. Stable air, on the other hand, is less able to go over the peninsula, so produces stronger corner effects.

Reflecting and diffracting

A fluid moving toward a solid obstacle that it cannot simply move over or around will be reflected backwards. This is seen when water beats against a shoreline abutment or a steep-sided cliff with no shallow beach in front of it. The water is thrust backwards against the incoming flow, creating turbulent, chaotic seas. Winds respond in a similar fashion when they hit directly into a headland, causing turbulent eddies. In some situations the fluid may actually be diffracted around the end of a jetty or similar object, causing waves to spread into the shadow zone behind it.

When sitting at the edge of a river I saw a small wood chip, bobbing slightly as the stream pushed it steadily toward a rock. But it was held in one place by what must have been an equally strong eddy reflected off the rock. A light craft such as a kayak might experience a similar effect if caught between a forward moving current and an eddy.

Upwelling and overfalls

Another example of reflection, but this time not of surface fluid movements, but of movements near the ocean floor, results in "upwelling." When a strong current passes over submerged ridges or shoals the water is forced upward. This can result in a dome of colder water at the surface. Dramatic drops in water level may result just downstream of the upwelling, creating severe "overfalls."

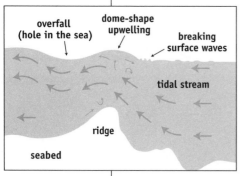

Upwelling over an obstacle on the sea bottom.

Upwelling may also develop by water being drawn upward, when water is removed at the surface. The most noticeable example of this occurs off the California coast. In summer with strong northwest winds, coriolis forces cause the water to move to the right, away from the coast. Cold water from the depths below is drawn upward to replace the surface waters. Water temperatures off central and southern California may be as cold in the summer, or even colder, than off the BC coast. Southerly winds off the Peruvian coast (with coriolis forces causing movement to the left in the southern hemisphere) also result in upwelling of cold waters. This has gained worldwide attention since El Niño episodes result in a weakening of the southerly winds, which in turn ends the upwelling of cold waters. Upwelling occurs along the west side of the Queen Charlotte Islands and Vancouver Island with northwest winds, and along the east side of the Charlottes with southerly winds, but in these situations the upwelling is more intermittent and less developed.

Rainbelts and rain shadows

Air movement also experiences its own type of upwelling when it encounters hills and mountains, or the "soft" frontal boundary of cold air, and is forced upward. It can also be drawn upward by divergence of winds aloft, but this is more a phenomenon of weather system development rather than one of local effects. Coastal water upwelling results in nutrient-rich waters being brought up

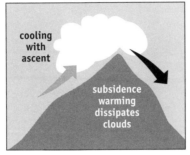

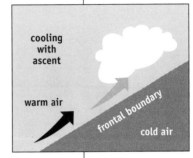

Air movement experiences its own type of upwelling when it encounters hills and mountains and is forced upward.

from the depths. Upward air movement, on the other hand, results in the formation of clouds. The expression of this upward motion is the enhanced precipitation that occurs on windward facing slopes. The corresponding effect to the downward flow of overfalls is a thinning of cloud due to subsidence warming, and a rain shadow within the area of precipitation. Both the windward enhancement and the leeside rain shadow can be seen on the map of annual precipitation in Chapter 4.

Downslope winds

Another parallel between overfalls caused by water flow over a subsea ridge, and air flow over a mountain ridge is a katabatic, or downslope wind. When the air is stable, but the winds are strong, some of the air blowing over the ridge will drop down onto the sea, while the remainder of the airstream aloft continues moving downstream. This downslope wind can be strengthened after a front has crossed the ridge. The winds will be sucked into the lower pressure near the front, and will be pushed by the rapidly rising pressures behind it.

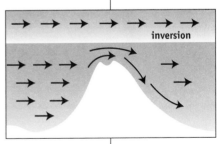

The winds trapped in this mountain-top layer increase in speed as they are thrust down the mountains and onto the sea.

The winds can be even stronger if there is an inversion above the mountain (i.e. when the temperature is warmer aloft) that acts as a boundary preventing the winds from dissipating by spreading upward. The winds trapped in this mountaintop layer increase in speed as they are thrust down the mountains and onto the sea. This is similar to when a stream flows past a rock that is lying just below the surface of the water. The moving water forms a bow-shaped wave over the rock, then plunges down as it passes the rock. Downslope winds can come up very quickly and reach speeds of 40 to 50 knots, but fortunately do not usually last much longer than an hour or two before the pressure difference is equalized and the force behind the wind dies away.

Downstream eddies

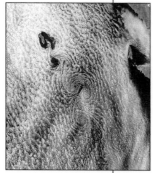

When winds flow around a large island that has significant topography and is isolated from other topographical features, then the flow is strengthened on the left side of the island (when the wind is at your back), and reduced on the right side, due to convergence, divergence, and corner effects. Eddies also develop near the lee edge of the island. A mariner normally would not see the eddies but would only experience gusty conditions. If there was sufficient moisture in the air the movements would be shown in the clouds that form in the upward motions. The classic example of this occurs when air flows around a solitary mountain, setting up a series of eddies that start at the base of the mountain and extend for miles downstream. The stream of vortices that results is called "von Karman vortices," named after Theodore von Karman who first observed the phenomenon. The picture was taken on 20 August 1999.

Crossing waves

Eddies form in water flow around islands if the speed and angle are right, but more often the lee side of islands produces "crossing waves" through refraction of the wave trains around the island. Crossing waves may also develop when swells interact with locally generated wind waves or with swells from a different direction. The seas in crossing waves develop pyramidal shapes with short, sharp wave crests, and appear confused.

Waves bend around an island to create "crossing waves."

Temperature and salinity effects

The coast lies at the boundary between the two realms of water and land. Moving water and air cannot penetrate physical objects so are forced to go around or over them. Heat, on the other hand, can and does penetrate physical objects and modifies their temperature. Rock, soils, and trees cover our land surface, and they all heat up faster than water. As a result, for approximately half a year, from April to September, the coastal water is colder, on average, than the land, while the water is warmer than the land from October to March. These temperature differences are the main driving force for a circulation of air between the two. Within the realms of both air and water, circulations are also created wherever there are temperature differences, since temperature affects the density of them both. Air, and to a large extent water, are both more dense when cold. Salinity also plays a somewhat lesser role in water circulations, as salt water is more dense than fresh.

Land and sea breezes

Land and sea breezes are the best known circulations caused by temperature differences. When the air over land is heated more rapidly than the air over the adjacent water surface, the warmer air rises, and the relatively cool air from the sea flows onshore to replace it. As the day progresses the sea breeze circulation gradually strengthens and extends back farther offshore, as well as farther inland. Winds with speeds of 10 to 15 knots can extend 15 miles out to sea by late afternoon. The wind will generally veer as it strengthens. During the evening the sea breeze rapidly subsides. At night, as the land cools, a land breeze develops in the opposite direction, and flows from the land out over the water. It is generally not as strong as the sea breeze, but can be gusty.

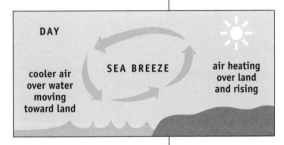

Land and sea breezes are the best known circulations caused by temperature differences.

Valley winds

Temperature differences between sunny and cloudy areas can also cause winds to blow from the cloudy to the warmer, sunny areas. Valley winds are caused by differences in heating between air over the valley bottom (or the inlet waters) and the mountain slopes. An upslope (anabatic) wind begins when the slopes of the valley or inlet start to warm up and the air over them begins to rise. The rising air is replaced by air coming up from the inlet or valley bottom. The strength of the upslope wind increases until the slopes reach their maximum temperature. Gently sloped valley sides, especially those facing south, are heated more strongly than those of a steep, narrow inlet. As a result, valley breezes will be stronger in the wider valleys. Upslope winds end soon after the heating stops.

Drainage winds are generally stronger than daytime upslope winds.

Drainage (katabatic) winds begin as mountain slopes cool during the evening, and the air immediately adjacent to the slopes becomes colder. The cooling of the mountain slopes occurs faster than the cooling of the air within the valley. This layer of cool air is initially very thin but increases in depth as the night goes on. When the layer becomes thick enough to flow over the bushes and shrubs of the forest slope, it starts to move down the mountainside. Often it may hold up in flatter parts of the slopes until its depth increases, as it is added to by streams of cold air coming from other sources farther up the mountain. Like many rivulets rushing into a stream, it eventually builds and moves faster down the slope, and out into the flat bottom of the valley floor, or over the inlet of the sea. This last rush of the cold air often comes suddenly, as if a dam had broken. Drainage winds are generally stronger than the daytime upslope winds. The water equivalent of a sea breeze and valley winds can be seen in closed inlets, and on a grander scale in global ocean circulations.

Internal waves

Within the ocean, boundaries can develop between two water bodies or streams that have different properties. Temperature and salinity are the main distinguishing factors between the two bodies. Since each water body has its own motions there will be waves, called "internal waves," that develop along the boundary between them. Internal waves often develop in areas where fresh water from river runoff overrides salt water.

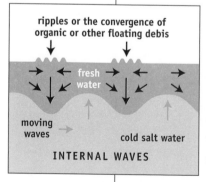

INTERNAL WAVES

Water movement associated with the passage of an internal wave is similar to movement within the atmosphere. Water moves down from the crest of the wave into the trough. Circulating flows are set up, which may have a reflection on the surface. This surface reflection is usually in the form of alternating bands of disturbed water, called slicks, with smooth bands of undisturbed water in between. Internal waves will only be visible on the surface when there are no wind waves or swell present.

Since each water body has its own motions there will be waves, called "internal waves," that develop along the boundary between them.

Water waves "feeling" the coast

The most obvious impact of the coast on moving water is that it undergoes four related changes when it begins to "feel" the bottom. While they are some of the most important coastal effects, they have been saved until the end for they are a perfect lead-in to a discussion on weather systems. To understand the changes that are created, however, requires a reminder about moving waves. It was mentioned earlier that waves can be of two types: progressive, in which the form of the wave moves but the water only rotates in small circles and doesn't move forward with the wave; and stationary, in which the form remains stationary, but the water moves forward.

The first of the changes is caused by a line of waves approaching the coast and being "refracted" until the waves move straight onto the beach. Initially the line of waves may approach the beach on a sharp angle but the end of

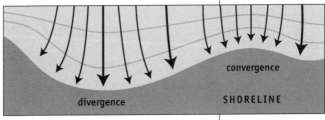

the line that is closest to the shore is slowed more than the end that is farther offshore, so the line rotates gradually until it becomes parallel with the beach. All the individual waves then move perpendicularly onto the beach. This refraction of the moving line of waves causes the waves to focus around headlands and submarine ridges, and to fan out over bays and submarine canyons.

Waves converging around headlands and diverging in bays.

The second change occurs when a waveform moves into shallow water encountering greater and greater friction as it begins to feel the bottom. (It feels bottom when the water depth is about one half of the length of the wave.) This frictional effect slows the motion of the wave. But since the waves in deeper water have not begun to feel the bottom to the same extent, they continue to move at their original speed. These faster moving waves catch up to those that are ahead and bunch up, so to speak, making the waves steeper, higher, and closer together. This process is called "shoaling," and may take place over offshore seamounts, as well as along coastal beaches.

"Shoaling" makes the waves steeper, higher, and closer together.

The above changes refer to the movement of the waveforms, but water in the waves also undergoes changes. A part of the shoaling process is the final

Water in the wave moves in circular motions offshore, but flattens into an ellipse as it moves up the beach.

breaking of the waves. When the wave moves up the beach it is slowed more and more at the bottom of the wave, but the top is slowed less, and eventually tumbles over ahead of the base. The form of the breaking wave varies with the shape of the beach itself.

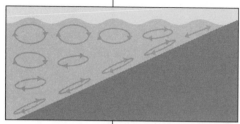

The fourth and last change also involves the movement of water within the waveform. As waves move into the shallow water of a beach, the waveform moves onward until it is dissipated by the coast. The water in the wave moves in circular motions offshore, but flattens into an ellipse and finally changes to simple forward and backward motions - the ebb and flow of the waves - as it moves up the beach.

Weather systems "feeling" the coast

Weather systems, being themselves waves in the westerly flow, are transformed in a similar way to waves moving up a beach. The winds and weather associated with the weather systems are akin to the motion of water within the waves. When a weather system approaches the coast there is a stream of air that moves up against the coast. The stream is slowed by friction with the coast, while the air farther upstream is not, therefore the airstream undergoes a "bunching-up" of air at the base of the mountains. This bunching-up, or "damming", is relieved somewhat by the fact that some of the stream is deflected by the mountains and flows along parallel with them, and some is able to pass over the top. But even then, there is an accumulation of air along the windward edge of the coastal mountains, resulting in a "windward ridge"

The front acts like a line of waves approaching the coast; it will slowly become parallel with the coast if it has enough time prior to crossing the coast.

of high pressure. Since only a portion of the air approaching the mountain actually moves over to the downwind or lee side, the air pressure on the lee side is lower than on the windward side. This area of lower pressure is called a "lee trough."

➜ **Diagram of windward ridge and lee trough.**

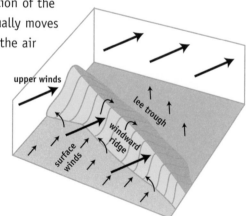

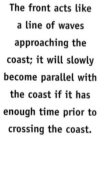

It should be remembered that as a weather system approaches the BC coast the lowest level winds are being steered by the terrain to become southeasterlies, but at higher levels the winds are not as strongly slowed by friction, so they flow directly toward the mountain from the southwest. It is these winds above the surface friction boundary level (about 1 km) that are forced upward over the mountain, causing increased amounts of cloud and rainfall during the ascent.

As the weather system approaches the coast the area of cloud first expands in size. The system then weakens as the upper winds leave the surface weather features behind. This sequence can be observed on satellite picture loops. The entire process is a reflection of the sequence of ocean waves bunching up along the coast, then as the tops of the waves move onward faster and finally break, the wave collapses and dies. These transformations show that weather systems are dynamic, ever-moving processes, and are not simple objects that move from place to place, without changing.

HIGHS, LOWS, FRONTS, AND RIDGES

The atmosphere, with its many layers of air, is in continual movement, and out of this movement, forms are created. The forms are not fixed and static, like a piece of sculpture, but breathe, develop, and change, like music. And as with classical music, which follows patterns, even if they are not always evident to the untrained ear, the atmosphere has its own repertoire of patterns. The purpose of this chapter is to look at some of these patterns, to understand the movements that created them, to see how they move over the offshore waters, and how they change as they encounter the BC coast.

Highs, lows, fronts, and ridges are the names of these forms, which are often referred to as "weather systems." The word "system" is defined as a combination of parts of a whole. But lows and highs are more than a collection of parts, they are an interweaving of processes. The word organism comes closer perhaps, for its definition includes the phrase, "interdependent parts." By whatever name they are called, they have a certain life cycle; they are born, they live for a while, then they die. But what is a high, a low, a front, a ridge? And how do their forms develop?

A low pressure system is sometimes called a mid-latitude cyclone, a "disturbance," a "depression," or simply, a "storm."

47

Surface weather maps

As you stand on earth the entire weight of the atmosphere is upon you. You can imagine rays of the sun streaming toward the earth, the upper layers of the atmosphere reaching out toward it, and the earth below affecting the lower layers. Continuous movement takes place in between. The weight that presses down on you, which you measure with a barometer, is the summation of all these movements and influences. If you move to a different location, you will experience a different pressure value, for the atmosphere's movements are different there. After the passage of time you will again experience a different pressure, for the atmospheric motions have again changed.

The surface weather map plots the variations in pressure that occur over a region of the map. Each spot on this map shows the end result of all movements in the air above that spot. An area where the pressure is higher is called a "high pressure system," or simply a "high." Likewise an area with lower pressure is called a "low pressure system," or "low." The map does not outline either of these features, saying that this is the area covered by a high, or this is the area of a low. Only their centres are marked, for there is no definition of where a high ends, or a low begins. They are but relative variations within the field of pressure. A "ridge of high pressure" (usually just called a "ridge"), and a "trough of low pressure," or "trough," are areas of relatively higher or lower pressure, and do not have complete circular rotations. The lines on a surface map are called isobars, and are simply lines joining places with equal pressure. The closer these lines are together, the greater the pressure difference is across that area.

Early weather map for 14 March 1904 →

The modern weather map, which displays pressure variations and other weather elements for a specific area, at a set time, was only possible after the invention of the telegraph. The telegraph allowed the data to be gathered in near-real time. The first public display of the early "synchronous charts," as they were originally called, was made during the Great Exhibition in London, in 1851.

As individuals we remain in one location, and the panorama of weather passes us by, through the course of time. Weather maps and satellite pictures, on the other hand, display the entire sequence of weather, over a large region in space, for one moment in time. Weather is a phenomenon of both time and space.

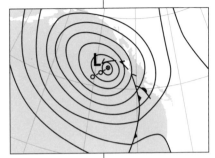

This surface weather map for 1700 hours 16 May 2002 is accompanied by a three-dimensional representation of its pressure field. The higher pressure is seen as an upward bulge in the pressure field, and the low, a downward depression.

Weather varies dramatically from place to place over the earth, both in the global and micro-scale. Clouds are seen as objects in space, while in reality they are but the expressions of movements through time. Highs, lows, fronts, and ridges are not physical forms in space, but are movement-forms written into the invisible air, through time. By keeping this in mind, weather becomes a dynamic process, rather than a collection of static facts.

Basic wind movement within highs and lows

What about the dynamics, the movements, that take place in the atmosphere to create areas of high and low pressure? What are the movements within the high and the low? Observations plotted on the surface weather map show that winds blow around the low in a counter-clockwise fashion, and blow slightly in toward the centre. This produces an inward spiralling vortex. Similarly, winds blow clockwise around the high, creating an outward moving spiral. But if the air is continually spiralling into the low, why doesn't it fill up, so to speak, as the pressure gradually rises with the added weight of the incoming air? The answer to this requires a look at the process involved in the creating of a low.

Fronts

If the flow of winds across the earth was everywhere the same, if it was uniform in time and space, then no low would form. But because of the rotation of the earth, and unequal heating of its surface, the flow is not uniform. Stronger and weaker streams of air develop. And as seen earlier in the example of a river, rotational shearing develops where a strong flow lies adjacent to a weaker flow. Since these two moving streams have different properties, boundaries develop between them. These boundaries were given the name "front" by a 1920's Norwegian meteorologist, Wilhelm Bjerknes. Temperature is the main property that distinguishes the merging streams.

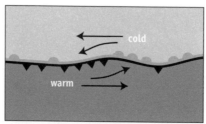

When two streams of air converge at an angle, some of the air is forced upward. If this upward moving air spreads outward aloft, then the pressure through the column of air above the convergence is reduced. Thus the two streams create a trough of low pressure along the line where they converge. A front always lies in a trough, just like a river is always found in a valley. The boundary between two fluids will persist only as long as the properties of the two fluids remain distinct. Continuous and rapid movement within the two fluids limits any significant exchange between them. Once they do merge, however, and become unified, the boundary ceases to exist.

A front always lies in a trough just like a river is always found in a valley.

Development of a low

The stage is now set for the development of a low. The two airstreams, or masses, are moving at different speeds, and have a frontal boundary between them. The shearing motion between these streams causes a rotation to begin.

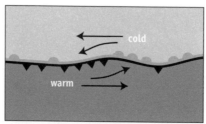

1. Wave develops - fronts begin moving

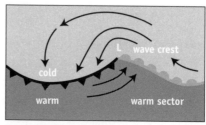

2. Low pressure forms

3. Wave/low moves along front

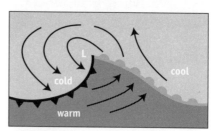

4. Mature low

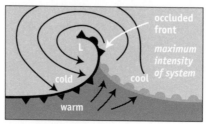

5. Warm air occludes

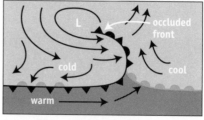

6. Low fills - warm air retracts

This rotation shows itself as a slight buckling, or waving, on the front. The two streams, like the flow in the river, do not stop moving when the rotation begins. The rotation-induced wave simply ripples along the front between the two moving airstreams.

In the northern hemisphere, the air in the warmer stream, being lighter, moves upward and toward the north, once the rotation begins. The cold airstream moves southward, and undercuts the warm air. These two encircling motions combine to create upward motion. Most of the dynamics of the low are now present. The only other thing required is a certain flow pattern aloft. If the air converging into the developing low were to move upward, but remain in the column above the low, then the total weight of air in the column would increase, the surface pressure would rise, and the low would begin to fill. For a low to continue to develop, the rising air has to be removed from above the low. The air aloft continually streams over the developing low, but if it is a steady stream then the weight of the air in the column remains the same. What is needed is a diverging of the air aloft so that it spreads out in different directions. A converging airstream aloft, on the other hand, would cause the volume of air to increase above the low, and would result in the surface low filling rapidly.

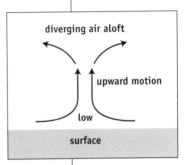

Diverging air above a low.

Once the pressure falls at the surface, the circulation strengthens, and more and more air spirals into the centre of the low - at low levels. Throughout this time the wave continues to ripple along the front. The development continues until the colder air completes a full circle, fully pinching off the warm air, so that it is only found aloft. This warm air is then said to be "occluded." The low has become detached from the front, and is only connected by the trough of warm air that persists aloft. This upper trough is called a "trowal" in Canada (short for TRough Of Warm Air aLoft), but is also referred to as an "occluded front." The low then spins itself out and dies, since it no longer has the dynamics of air flowing into it.

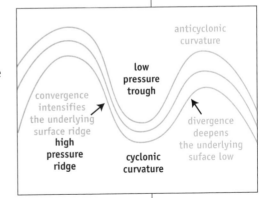

Pattern of flow aloft and changes in surface weather features.

Development of a high

The formation of a high is not generally given as much thought, for it often forms as a result of the low development, rather than a development on its own. The low is often referred to as a "storm" for it brings both wind and rain. A high, on the other hand, generally brings clearer skies, so even if it does create strong winds at times, it is looked on with more favour. When a large clockwise buckle does form in the flow aloft, a surface ridge can develop. The surface ridge will grow strongly if the air in this flow aloft is converging. A high can be seen as an attempt by the atmosphere to return to its desired equilibrium. It is a balancing, or compensation, for the development of a low.

3D motions within a low

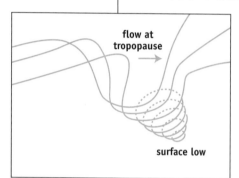

flow at
tropopause

surface low

The full flow can only be shown by a series of flowing streams that occur at all levels from the surface up to the tropopause.

One other way of viewing the movement of air into and around a low is based on a study of the flow of winds at different levels, from the surface up to the tropopause. At the surface, in a well-developed low, there is a strong circulation of air spiralling inwards. But the flow near the tropopause doesn't show a complete rotation, except with the strongest of lows. Instead, the upper flow normally has a large trough just west of the surface low, with strong southwest winds ahead of it, and strong northwest winds behind. At some point between the surface and the tropopause, the spiralling circulation opens up into a trough - with no westward moving flow north of the trough. Following the movement of an individual air particle will not show all of the movements within the full depth of the low. This can only be shown by a series of flowing streams that occur at all levels from the surface up to the tropopause.

The transition from the wavelike flow in the upper levels of the troposphere, to the closed circulation at the surface is the same transition in space as that which takes place over time, with the development of a low from a weak frontal wave to a deep surface low.

The motions within highs and lows, and along frontal boundaries can be seen in satellite pictures. They are not seen directly, but only by the clouds that result from the motion. Clouds form where the air is moist and ascending, and are not visible in areas of dry descending air.

Centres of action

"Centres of action" is a term that has been given to sets of semi-permanent high and low pressure systems that develop in the global circulation, in more or less fixed locations on earth. They are linked to the topography of their surroundings. The two features are connected, and work as couplets, for each one's individual development and movement influences the other. In the Pacific Ocean, the low pressure centre of action is found near the Aleutian Islands, in the northern Gulf of Alaska. Its counterpart is the "Pacific high" found off the California coast. In the Atlantic, the low pressure centre of action is near Iceland, with the high being found near the Azores Islands. There is one other centre of action couplet in the northern hemisphere, but in this case the two parts are not separated in space, but in time. In winter a huge high develops over Asia, but this high changes in summer to an intense low. The Pacific and Atlantic centres of action are united by flow across the space between them; the Asian centres are united through the course of time.

Seasonal variations of the centres of action

The Aleutian low is not a permanent feature like the sub-tropical high, nor is it a single low that is found only near the Aleutian Islands. It is instead a graveyard for lows, an area into which low pressure systems repeatedly move, where they remain for periods of time, and where they eventually die, before being replaced by other lows arriving from farther west. In autumn, the strength and frequency of lows moving into the northern Gulf of Alaska increases and reaches its peak in early November. The sub-tropical high, on the other hand, is at its most compressed form in winter. It generally lies between 25° and 35°N, just off the California coast, but may at times retreat inland, over the southwestern USA.

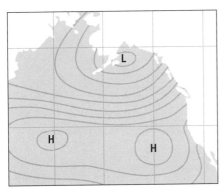

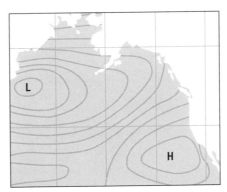

OCTOBER   **JANUARY**

In the spring, as the sun rises higher in the sky and the warmer water temperatures spread northward, the high first builds westward, off the coast, then farther north. It reaches its maximum northern extent in late July, before it shrinks back southward again, following the path of cooling ocean waters. It moves closer to the North American coast as autumn passes, and again finds its winter home either off the Baja Peninsula, or over the southwestern States.

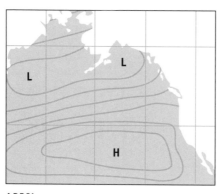

APRIL

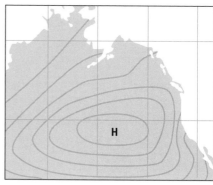

JULY

Jet streams

The presence and movement of the sub-tropical high determines where the band of prevailing westerlies to its north will occur, and influences the strength of

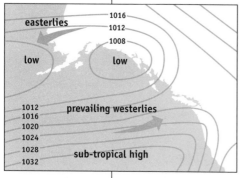

The jet stream reflects the flowing movements of the westerlies.

the westerlies. The stream of winds near the tropopause, called the jet stream, reflects the flowing movements of the westerlies. This stream, like the rivers that move across the land, does not flow for any length of time in a ruler-straight line but oscillates in waves, back and forth. The jet stream can develop such significant meanders that the orientation of the stream is no longer from east to west, but almost north-south. When the jet stream flow buckles this much, the flow is called "meridional," for it follows the direction of the meridian lines of longitude. In contrast to this, the regular east-west flow is called "zonal."

The jet stream varies in strength through the year, for the pressure contrast between the high to the south and the low in the north is much stronger in winter than in summer. The jet stream tends to be more zonal in October, November, and early December, and as a result, the developing weather systems move steadily one after the other onto the coast. Things tend to change in

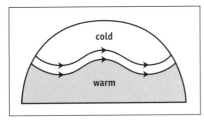

ZONAL FLOW

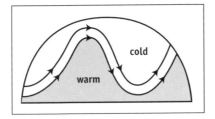

MERIDIONAL FLOW

mid-to late December, and more so again in early spring, when meridional patterns become common. A meridional, or blocking pattern, results in the persistence of one particular type of weather for days. The weather that is experienced in any location depends on where the upper ridge or trough is located. If the surface ridge is to the west of the coast, there will be north-west winds and showery conditions. If the ridge is east of the coast, over the BC interior, then days of dry outflow winds can be expected. But if the ridge is too far west or east, then a trough of low pressure that develops ahead of the ridge will bring days of cloud, and rain or drizzle.

Secondary waves, or eddies, that form in the lower layers of the atmosphere are called "short waves," to distinguish them from the much bigger, "long" waves of the jet stream meanders. Most weather systems that bring strong winds and rain to the coast start as short waves, but if they develop significantly, they modify the shape and path of the jet stream itself. When short waves move through a long-wave trough they strengthen; but when they move through a long-wave ridge, they weaken.

Sea surface temperatures

The movement of the sub-tropical high is not the only reflection of the sun moving higher in the sky in the spring, and lowering again in the autumn. The temperatures of the global seas also show the same yearly breathing rhythm. In recent years much attention has been given to changes in the sea surface temperatures (SST), for the El Niño and La Niña phenomena have clearly shown that there is a strong connection between global water temperatures and weather. The following maps show the average SST for the months of October, January, April, and July.

The unusual autumn 2002 weather in which weather systems were kept well off the coast had a very marked meridional jet stream pattern that persisted for many weeks. It moved or weakened periodically but kept reforming again.

Hammerhead sharks and a Great White shark were seen in Johnstone Strait, and anchovy, tuna, and sunfish were caught offshore during the warm water period of the 1997/1998 El Niño. The seasonal salmon run was also delayed by six weeks during this time, and the waters off the central coast became turquoise in colour.

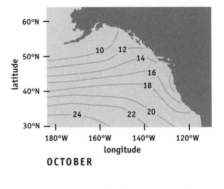

OCTOBER

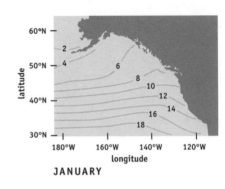

JANUARY

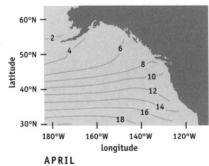

APRIL

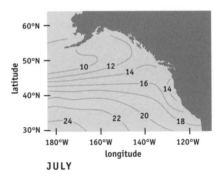

JULY

Average yearly sea surface temperatures at Pine Island from 1950 to 2000.

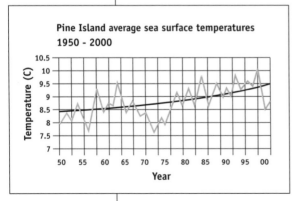

The graph shows the average yearly sea surface temperatures at Pine Island from 1950 to 2000. While there are many ups and downs through these years, the trend line, marked in black, shows that the average water temperature has risen from about 8.5°C to near 9.5°C during this period. Following a 21 year period that saw temperatures above normal, the highest value was recorded in 1997. It then fell sharply in 1999, and has remained low ever since. The reasons for these changes are not known, but may be part of a North Pacific sea surface temperature cycle called the Pacific Decadal Oscillation.

Tracks of Pacific weather systems

The developing lows generally form on the north side of the jet stream. This means that if the jet stream is well north, then the lows will track close to the Aleutian Islands before moving into the Gulf of Alaska. If the jet stream is farther south, then the lows may cross the coast as a coastal low before they are able to turn north into the Gulf of Alaska.

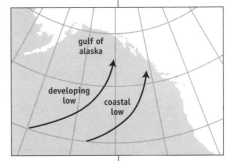

The developing lows generally form on the north side of the jet stream.

The world ocean is one continuous body of water that has no boundaries between its parts, but is often divided into four basins, the Pacific, Atlantic, Indian, and Arctic. Many use the word "sea" interchangeably with the word "ocean," but according to the International Hydrographic Bureau, a sea is a subdivision of an ocean, and they suggest that there are 54 seas worldwide. Within the Mediterranean region there are seven seas, the Adriatic, Aegean, Balearic, Ligurian, Tyrrhenian, Ionian, and the Mediterranean. A sailor could sail the seven seas, but never venture onto an ocean!

When there is a straight line, west-to-east upper flow, with no buckles of ridges or troughs, the systems move fairly rapidly and will be relatively weak. In the autumn, after the quiet days of early September, the intensity and strength of approaching lows increases dramatically. During this period many of the lows are the remnants of tropical storms that developed off the Asian coast then weakened over the colder waters of the north Pacific. Sometimes they seem to disappear altogether during their crossing over the Pacific, then redevelop again as they move toward the BC offshore waters. These low-pressure systems often move at speeds of 30 to 40 knots.

In an El Niño year there is often a ridge of high pressure near the BC coast that causes a split in the flow, with one jet stream going north over the Alaska Panhandle while a second jet stream heads south toward California. In a La Niña year the jet stream tracks over the BC coast and may result in lows moving across the coast, as coastal lows.

The Pacific Ocean is the largest of the world's oceans. It occupies nearly one third of the earth surface and its total area is more than all land masses combined.

Lows can develop anywhere across the Pacific within the belt of prevailing westerlies. When they develop off the Asian coast they generally move eastward across the dateline between 35° and 50°N. The lows curve more sharply toward the north once they begin to deepen. This deepening and curving northward often takes place between 160° and 140°W. Once the low starts to develop, pressures fall rapidly, the size of the system increases, and wind speeds rise. The lows and associated fronts are frequently spaced about 1500 to 2500 nautical miles apart, and as a result arrive on the coast every 1½ to 3 days.

Summary

The changes that can be seen and experienced as water interacts with the physical coastline are mirrored in the changes that air undergoes when it encounters the topography. You can learn a lot about air movements by looking at the movements of water.

Returning to the original question, what are highs, lows, and fronts? The answer is that they are "forms" that arise from movement of air. These forms are invisible to the eye, but are the basic organs of weather. Their reflection is seen on surface weather maps and in satellite pictures. Within these forms air moves, creating wind, clouds, and rain. Weather systems are both the result of movement, and the creator of movement.

The movements and changes in intensity of weather systems are described in the synopsis of the marine forecast. Take note of these descriptions for they give indications of the timing and strength of the approaching weather systems. Try to picture the wind patterns that accompany the weather systems and imagine how these patterns will change as the system moves. Listen to subsequent forecasts for any changes in the tracks and intensity of the systems. The forecast movements are just that, forecasts, and with later information the descriptions may need to change.

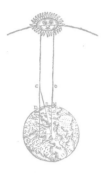

German scientist Athanasius Kircher discovered which parts of the globe would be light and which dark at a given time of year.

the four winds

EASTERLY, NORTHERLY, SOUTHERLY, WESTERLY

PRESSURE-SLOPE EXPLANATION

THIS CHAPTER is another step on the path of increasing practical knowledge that will lead toward a greater understanding of weather across the BC coast.

Here the pressure-slope concept is developed into a working tool that will enable the many variations of weather patterns to be grouped into five distinct categories. These five categories consist of the four primary winds: easterly, northerly, southerly, and westerly, plus the fifth group, the coastal low, which potentially includes them all.

The ordering of the winds that is used is not the usual rotation around the compass from north to east, south, then west, nor does it follow the opposite rotation from north, west, south, then to east. It also does not follow the cycle that has been fixed into our English word for information passing, the NEWS. The order of wind directions is rather a reflection of the change of seasons, beginning in autumn, and then passing through winter, spring and summer. In autumn, which is considered here to be from mid to late September through to the same time in December, the dominant wind is from the east, which because of the orientation of our coastline frequently means southeasterlies. During winter, easterly winds still prevail, but the season is distinguished from autumn by the occasional presence of northerly outflow winds. Within the months of spring the winds shift from the dominant easterly and northerly winds of autumn and winter, to the westerly winds of summer. During this transition period southerly winds are common.

COASTAL PRESSURE-SLOPE

The pressure-slope concept is used as a tool to identify the weather patterns that create the four main winds. It is also used to distinguish the variations that can take place in each wind category. The pressure-slope is an aid in the visualization of changes that can take place with different weather systems, but is not intended to be an absolute statement about when certain winds will occur. The use of this tool may help to distinguish between patterns that create winds that seriously affect a region, from those that don't.

↑
The pressure-slope icon in the upper corner of each page indicates the wind direction that is under discussion.

EASTERLY

NORTHERLY

SOUTHERLY

WESTERLY

COASTAL LOW

OVERVIEW

How to use the pressure-slope indications

Copy the compass onto a plastic overlay. This overlay can be used over maps that are obtained from a radio weatherfax, or from the internet.

→

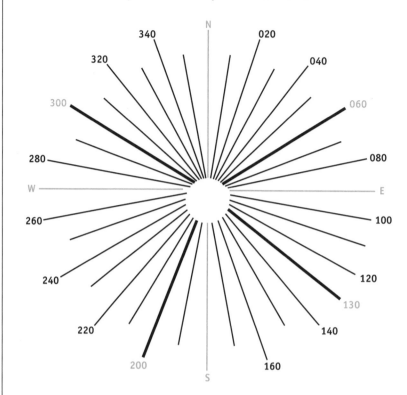

Keep in mind that there are two types of weather maps: analysis and forecast maps. Always note the valid time of the map, remembering that the time is often given in Universal Coordinated Time (UTC), or Greenwich Mean Time (GMT) and is sometimes abbreviated with the letter Z. Analyzed maps are generally done every six hours, at 00, 06, 12, 18 UTC (1600, 2200, 0400, 1000 PST). Forecast maps may list both the valid time of the map, and the time that the map was created. In most cases the forecast maps are created twice a day, around 1200 and 0000 UTC. Use the latest map available.

GMT or UTC is 8 hours ahead of Pacific Standard Time (PST) and seven hours ahead of Pacific Daylight Time (PDT), e.g. UTC = PST + 8.

To determine the pressure-slope, place the centre of the overlay over the area of the weather map in question. Place a pencil or pen on the overlay in such a way that it is perpendicular to the isobars and pointing toward the centre of the overlay, so that it points from higher to lower pressure. The value of the compass number that is closest to the pencil line is the pressure-slope. If the

62

pencil runs along the compass radius labelled 060° then the pressure-slope is 060°, i.e. northeast. After an initial use of the overlay it might become possible to estimate the pressure-slope without it. It is simply a tool for learning.

Once the pressure-slope quadrant is determined the other factor to consider is the pressure-slope gradient (the spacing of the isobars). The pressure-slope gradient is a measure of the steepness, or intensity of the weather system. The higher the pressure-slope gradient, the stronger the potential winds. The strength of the associated winds is linked, however, with the pressure-slope direction itself, for the coastal topography influences which direction of wind is possible, and which isn't. In some coastal areas, the inlets for instance, the winds will be light in certain pressure-slope directions, no matter how strong the gradient. The winds may blow aloft, above the local terrain, but do not surface inside the inlets. Remember that when the pressure-slope gradient is weak, the winds may not conform to the normal pressure-slope schemes. During summer, which often has weak pressure gradients, the daytime heating and cooling may override pressure-slope considerations. Finally, it is good to keep in mind that some locations may have particular topographical surroundings that cause the winds to shift a little earlier or later than is general along the coast. The changes in wind direction usually take place within 10 degrees on either side of the main pressure-slope directions.

Weather maps show in space, what we may experience over time.

> A weather map shows the intensity of the weather system across a distance in space. It may show, for example, a pressure-slope gradient of 12 millibars over a distance of one hundred miles. But with the movement of the weather system we experience its intensity in time, as a fall in pressure of 12 millibars during a period of hours.

The pressure-slope variations in the examples that follow are illustrated with the use of three aids. One is a regular weather map with isobars and fronts. Another is a radar wind image that shows the surface roughness of the water, which indicates the wind speed. The third is a regular satellite picture.

FIVE BASIC WEATHER PATTERNS

1. Approaching front - *Easterly pressure-slope winds*

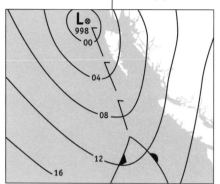

This pattern has a trough of low pressure offshore and a ridge to the east, along the Coast Mountains. A front normally lies within the trough. When a front approaches the coast the air flows into it and creates **easterly pressure-slope winds**. The orientation of the front and the local terrain influences the winds so that many places along the coast actually experience southeast winds.

2. Ridge over the interior - *Northerly pressure-slope winds*

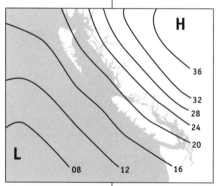

This pattern is similar to the first in that it has a trough of low pressure offshore and a ridge over the interior, but in this case the ridge is dominant and lies parallel with the Coast Mountains. The air is pushed out through the mainland inlets creating **northerly pressure-slope winds**. The actual wind direction that is observed depends on the orientation of the coastal topography, and can vary from northwest to east.

3. Coastal ridge - *Southerly pressure-slope winds*

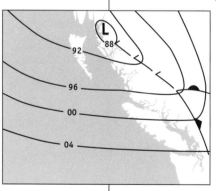

This pattern develops in one of two ways: when pressures rise sharply after the passage of a front, and when a ridge of high pressure develops on an east-west line across the coast, to the south of your location. The **southerly pressure-slope winds** are generally short lived as the pattern is normally one of transition. They are significant because they come from an uncommon direction, and as a result, are potentially dangerous.

4. Offshore ridge - *Westerly pressure-slope winds*

When a ridge of high pressure develops west of the coast the pressure is lower along the Coast Mountains, even though there may not be a well-defined

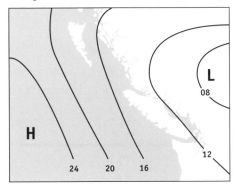

trough of low pressure there. The winds produced range from north-west to southwest directions and are generally referred to as **westerly pressure-slope winds**. Since this pattern frequently occurs during the summer it is linked to the time of diurnal wind effects.

5. Coastal low - *All pressure-slope wind directions*

This pattern occurs when a low develops so close to the coast that it doesn't have room to turn northward into the Gulf of Alaska before it passes over the

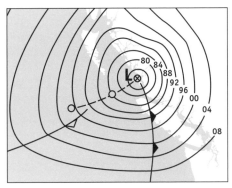

coast. The winds may be extreme close to the low centre. The wind direction changes around the low are affected by local topography. Knowledge of the exact track of the low is critically important. Lighter northerly winds are common north of its track, but gale to hurricane force southeast winds occur ahead of the low, south of the track.

EASTERLY WINDS

Easterly winds are dominant from late September through March.

Easterly winds can happen at any time of the year but are the dominant wind from late September through March. They develop ahead of an approaching low or associated front. While southeast winds are the main wind over most coastal waters ahead of a front, the word easterly is used because the actual direction of the wind varies with the local topography. Channels that run from east to west, such as Dixon Entrance and Queen Charlotte Strait, have winds that are more easterly than southeast. The inlets of the mainland coast, because of their orientation, have northeast winds, while the inlets of Vancouver Island are more northerly.

Since easterly winds rise to gale, storm, and even to hurricane force, they are a major concern for mariners. Such strong winds, combined with the large waves that they produce and the steady rain that accompanies them, are the ingredients of what most mariners simply call a storm.

Remember that conditions are always worse when winds blow against tidal currents.

The lows and fronts that create these storms vary in strength, orientation, and speed of motion. While each storm, or weather system, is slightly different as a result, they all can be simplified into two possible patterns, each of which then has other variations. The two patterns are based on the direction that the front arrives from, and its orientation. If a ridge of high pressure is over the coast, and the front approaches from the northwest, then the winds over the open waters back from west to south then southeast, and gradually strengthen. If the front approaches from the southwest then the winds start out from the northeast, but veer to east then to southeast, and gradually strengthen. In both cases the winds through the inlets remain from the northeast until near the passage of the front.

The pressure-slope reflects these changes. The pressure-slope ranges between southeast (130°) for the fronts coming from the northwest, to northeast (060°) for fronts coming from the southeast. In some years the lows tend to come more frequently from one or other of these two directions. Some indications suggest that lows tend to come more frequently from the northwest during El Niño years, and from the southwest during La Niña years.

Fronts that approach the coast from the northwest are associated with lows that turn into the northern Gulf of Alaska well before they approach the coast. The front moves away from the low, and first crosses the Queen Charlotte Islands before moving down the coast. Since the front weakens as it encounters land, the peak winds in the south will be less than in the north.

Fronts that approach the coast from the southwest are associated with lows that move close to the coast before turning northward, and in some cases, the low may actually cross the coast. The front in this instance will be oriented almost parallel with the coast so Vancouver Island will be as strongly impacted as the Queen Charlotte Islands, if not more so. The inlets will have stronger northerly winds ahead of a front coming from the southwest. The winds tend to shift more dramatically to the southwest after the frontal passage.

> The graphs in Chapter 1, under "The cycle of the year," show that the frequency of winds increases from mid-September to early December, then decreases after mid-December, when a ridge of high pressure strengthens over the BC interior. This drop in frequency of winds continues until mid-June, with many ups and downs along the way. The occasional pauses in the frequency of strong easterly winds seem to come at reasonably specific times of the year.

The strength of winds that occur depends on how close the low moves toward the coast, the strength, orientation, and speed of the front, and the position and strength of the high over the interior. If the low is deep and the ridge ahead of it is strong, then the pressure will drop and the winds will rise very rapidly with the approach of the front. A fast-moving system will also cause the pressure to fall more rapidly. When the pressure falls rapidly, it means the pressure-slope of the ridge-trough couplet is steep, and as a result, the winds will be strong. If the pressure change with the approach of the front is gradual, then the pressure-slope gradient will be low and the winds will not be as strong.

> The day before a big southeast storm is often deceptively calm - then it hits with a bang. Old-timers call these glassy calm days, "weather breeders."

One other factor, stability, will also affect the winds associated with an approaching front. Generally, stable air tends to produce lighter winds than less stable air, for it is not strengthened by the stronger flow above. But in coastal areas, the winds may actually be strengthened in stable conditions, since the flow of air may not be able to move up and over islands and

The *Minerva* was invented by a French balloonist named Etienne Robertson to carry 60 meteorologists and astronomers on a round-the-world voyage. It never left the ground.

67

peninsulas, but is strengthened through corner effects, as it passes around the edge of these obstacles. The air is most stable just ahead of the warm front and in the warm sector, between the warm front and the cold front. If the weather map shows a warm front just west of the coast, then you might expect that you will enter into the more stable air mass. This does not happen too often, because in most cases the warm air is pushed aloft by the encircling cold air, before the front crosses the coast. As a result, only the occluded front passes, with the warm air remaining above the surface. The warm front is often not detectable on satellite pictures.

Clouds and weather

With an approaching frontal system, the weather often progresses through a sequence of cloud forms. The first hint of the front is the appearance of cirrus.

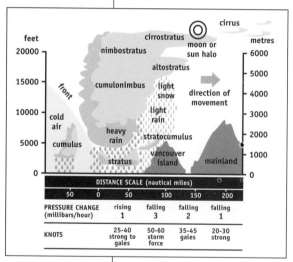

A generalized picture of clouds and weather associated with the approach of a strong front.

Occasionally it will first appear as lacy filaments or streaks, but more commonly during the autumn and winter it will appear as a gradually thickening veil of cirrostratus. It is hardly visible at first, only causing a slight whitening of the sky, but then as it thickens the blue of the clear sky is completely gone, and a white, featureless, overcast condition replaces it. The sun will initially shine through the cloud, but as it thickens a halo appears around the sun, with occasional "sun dogs" on either side, and then gradually the sun disappears completely. The clouds thicken further as the front approaches, and become lower and darker. The cirrostratus changes to altostratus and eventually to the dark, nimbostratus, rain clouds. As the rain becomes more intense, stratofractus clouds form in the rain, beneath the main clouds. The clouds thin and sometimes clear after the passage of the front. Cumulus, or cumulonimbus clouds develop, and give occasional showers if the air behind the front is cold and moist enough.

Seas

Ahead of the front, gale to storm force southeast winds may build the seas to 8 or 9 metres over the northern waters and to the west of Vancouver Island. In the intense storms the seas can reach 10 to 12 metres. Over the inner waters the seas are much lower due to sheltering from coastal land masses, and the sea height is largely controlled by the fetch distance. After the front crosses the coast, the winds usually decrease, the visibility improves, and the seas diminish. When the low tracks close to the coast, heavy swells, typically from 4 to 6 metres, arrive at the coast up to 12 hours after the front has passed. These waves form with the strong west or northwest winds on the western flank of the low.

Pressure-slope indications

The synthetic aperture derived wind images show the various speeds of winds across the region at the moment the picture was taken. Most images were taken just after 0200 UTC (1800 PST), although a few were taken at 1500 UTC (0700 PST). The wind speed scale at the bottom of the image shows that the lightest winds are dark blue, and then as the winds increase the colours change from light blue to yellow, and then to red. Areas of very light or calm winds are shown in black. The arrows marked over the images give the general wind direction, but they shouldn't be used to indicate the actual local winds as these vary with the local topography. It is interesting to note the areas where the winds are strong as well as where they are light. Much can be learned from both. While each weather system is unique these radar wind images do show patterns that are repeated time and time again.

In the first example of 29 June 2002, there is a plume of strong winds extending from Queen Charlotte Strait into southern Hecate Strait. These are southeast winds just ahead of the front. Note the plumes of strong easterly winds passing out the inlets on the Queen Charlotte Islands, and the areas of light winds between these plumes. Note also the areas of light winds inside the islands along the mainland coast. The area of light winds near the top of Vancouver Island represents the relative calm just behind the front. The area of strong winds to the southwest of Cape St. James, at the southern tip of the Charlottes, are the southwest winds that developed behind the front, close to the low.

A regular satellite picture is also included in each case, but it may not be for the same time as the radar wind image. Visual satellite pictures show much more detail than infrared pictures, so they were included even if they were one or two hours earlier or later than the radar wind image. Likewise, it should be noted that since weather maps are only made every six hours, the time of the analysis may not exactly correspond with the time of the satellite picture or the radar wind image.

". . .science always must be open-minded toward unexpected observations. Many surprises are without doubt in store for us, because we understand only parts of the whole."

KAREN LABITZKE
AND HARRY van LOON,
THE STRATOSPHERE

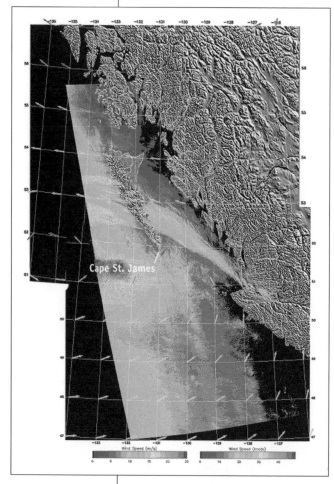

29 June 2002

The radar wind images for 29 June 2002 shows what the winds looked like as a front moved up from the southwest and passed over Hecate Strait. To the north of the front, the winds were light and from the east to northeast. Close to the front there was a band of stronger easterly winds that eventually moved right across the coast. Behind the front the winds shifted to southwest. The pressure-slope ranged from 020° in the north, to 100° over southern Hecate Strait ahead of the front, to near 180° behind the front. Note the strong easterly winds that poured out the inlets of the Queen Charlotte Islands, and the lighter winds between the inlets. Very strong southwest winds moved around the low and approached Cape St. James from the south. Fronts in the summer tend to be much weaker than their winter counterparts, but the patterns are the same.

The weather map and satellite image were for two hours before the time of the radar wind image. The front at that time was stretching from Cape St. James

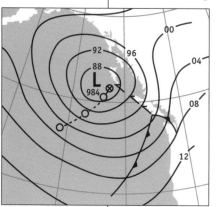

to the west coast of Vancouver Island. The low is located near the hook in the cloud on the satellite image southwest of Cape St. James.

A second example, from 13 October 2002, had a front approaching the Queen Charlotte Islands from the west. The southeast winds rose to gale force strength over northern Hecate Strait and in some places west of the Charlottes and northwest of Langara Island. The winds were lighter farther to the southeast, away from the low. Note the wind shadow near the top of Graham Island. where the winds were much lighter, but how they increased again toward the Alaska Panhandle. Note also that winds flowed almost parallel with the coast so the coastal areas of east Hecate Strait were generally sheltered, though some winds blew out from Grenville Channel. The pressure-slope was near 080°.

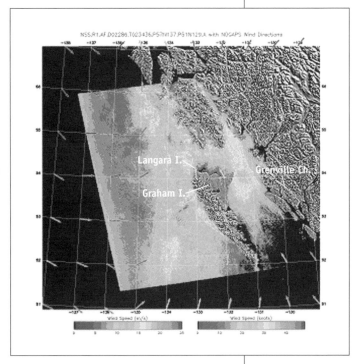

13 October 2002

The weather map, which was drawn two hours before the time of the radar wind image, shows the main low well north of the region with the front just west of the Queen Charlotte Islands. The satellite image shows a wave on the front and possibly a secondary low west of Langara Island. The band of cloud stretching south from Queen Charlotte Sound is low cloud that had been there well before the arrival of the front.

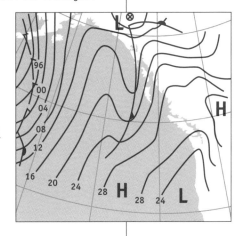

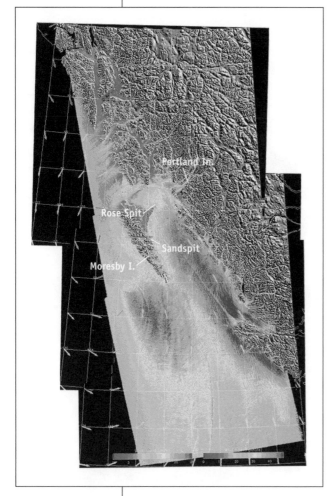

12 January 2002

A winter example of 12 January 2002, which again has a low approaching from the southwest, shows a large area of strong southeast winds across Hecate Strait that rose to storm force. A band of strong east to northeast winds that came out of the Portland Inlet has now been squeezed northward so that it only lies along the edge of the Alaska Panhandle. The pressure-slope in this case ranged from 040° in the north to 100 to 120° in the south. This image shows weaker winds and waves along the east side of Moresby Island due to lee shadowing by the island. These lighter winds are either an actual wind shadow, or just reduced water movement due to a limited fetch downwind of Moresby Island, or possibly a little of both. The lighter winds on the west side of Moresby Island are due to a relaxing of the pressure gradient just after the passage of the front. The stronger winds southwest of Cape St. James are caused by a strong gradient south of the low. Note also that strong winds are pouring through the channels along the mainland coastal edge.

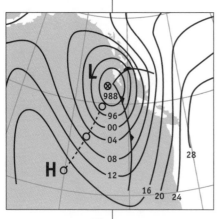

The low lies just west of Langara Island The front stretches along the western edge of the cloud that extends to the south of Cape St. James. The low is near the hook of cloud that wraps around the clear area west of the front.

In a situation when the low moves into the northern Gulf of Alaska and only the front passes over the coast, there wouldn't be this band of strong winds so close behind the front. Again note that the weather map and satellite image are valid two hours before the radar wind image.

When the pressure-slope is backed toward the northeast (about 060°) then the winds in Hecate Strait are stronger on the west side of the strait, and pour through Dixon Entrance and the inlets on the Charlottes as easterlies, but are light northeast along the mainland coast. When the pressure-slope veers beyond 090° the winds are stronger in the middle and eastern sections of Hecate Strait, and start increasing through the channels of the coastal edge. There will also be some lee shadowing along the Charlottes. At some point when the pressure-slope approaches 130° the winds could be equally strong on both sides of Moresby Island. The difference in angle between the pressure-slopes in these two examples is small, but the potential difference of winds at a given location may be dramatic.

> In general, the pressure-slope is closer to the southeast when the front comes from the Gulf of Alaska, and creates what could be called "true" southeast winds. When the front approaches from the southwest the pressure-slope will initially be from the northeast, and more easterly winds result.

If the first example was a more developed winter front, but still had a pressure-slope from the northeast, then the southeast winds would be strong all across the east side of the Charlottes. Then both Sandspit and Rose Spit would have equally strong winds. When the pressure-slope veers slightly more than in the second example, the lee shadow will spread up the Charlottes to Sandspit so that its winds will ease while Rose Spit winds remain strong.

> When viewed from the deck of a boat the subtle changes described may appear as nothing more than slight increases or decreases in wind strength. In some situations, however, knowing about some of the variations will help you understand why winds abruptly change, or don't change, when they are forecast to do so.

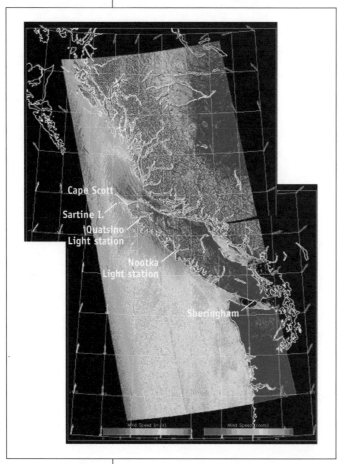

9 November 1999

The case of 9 November 1999 is a classic example of an autumn storm that gave hurricane force southeast winds near northwest Vancouver Island, with gale to storm force winds across the rest of the south coast. The pattern began on 8 November when a low moved into the Gulf of Alaska. This low weakened but a second low developed farther south and moved toward the Queen Charlotte Islands. At the time of this radar image the front is approaching northern Vancouver Island. The winds have already eased over the northern waters of Hecate Strait. The pressure-slope over Vancouver Island was 090°.

Note the fairly uniform area of strong winds that extend out Queen Charlotte Strait and up the west side of Vancouver Island. The winds at the time of this radar image ranged from 66 knots with gusts to 77 at Sartine Island, to five knots at Sheringham Pt. The direction of the wind was such that it blew into the inlets giving 60 knots at Quatsino lightstation, and 50 knots at Nootka. The winds were slightly lower over the southern areas. The seas in the inner waters were strongly limited by the fetch distance.

Note also the cone of lighter winds that lies between the winds moving up the west side of Vancouver Island, and those coming out Queen Charlotte Strait. This cone of lighter winds will be centred close to Cape Scott when the pressure slope is near 060°, but closer to the mouth of Queen Charlotte Strait when the pressure slope is near 130°. Cape Scott lies in this area of lighter southeast winds and as a result its wind reports are generally much less than what would be experienced on either side. Since the pressure-slope changes as the front passes, this cone of lighter winds moves and evolves over time, hence only provides a temporary place of shelter. Beyond this cone of lighter winds is a line of stronger winds caused by the converging of the two streams.

The front on the satellite image wraps around along the west edge of the cloud, from the low northwest of Langara Island to near Prince Rupert, then southward past Cape St. James.

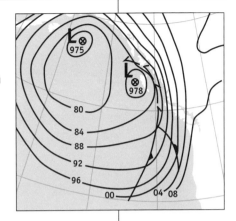

9 November 1999

October wind roses

The wind roses show the relative frequency of wind from each of the eight cardinal directions. The month of October is chosen to represent autumn, and its easterly winds. Winds in the inlets are primarily limited to blowing along the axes of the inlets. While southeast winds are the dominant wind direction in the more open waters, many other winds are also represented, especially west of the Queen Charlotte Islands. These variations are largely due to the fact that with each autumn storm the wind direction changes as the front approaches, then passes. It is most instructive to see how the wind roses vary from season to season. Topography always plays a role in steering the winds.

Wind direction
frequency
0-5	
5-10	
10-15	
15-20	
20-25	
25-30	
30-40	
40-50	
50-70	
70-100	

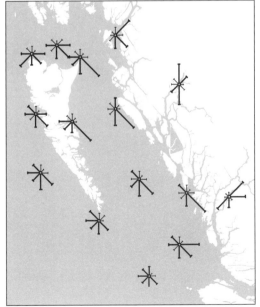

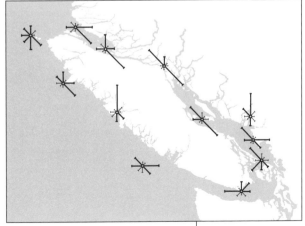

75

NORTHERLY WINDS

There are three basic types of northerly winds. The regular "garden variety" of northerlies occurs whenever there is a weak ridge of high pressure along the Coast Mountains, and a weak low or front offshore. These winds will rise to moderate to strong values, but are rarely dangerous. The ridge of high pressure that creates them is often a northern extension of the high that sits over Idaho and Montana through much of the winter.

Many mariners relish the idea of northerly winds, for when they occur the ridge over the interior is part of an upper air pattern that blocks the approach of other weather systems.

The second type of northerly winds develops when a high forms over the Yukon and northern BC, and builds southward into the central interior. This is the pattern that creates the strongest and most dangerous northerly winds - the arctic outflow. With high pressure over the interior during the winter the skies are clear and the temperature drops. The layer of cold air thickens over time, and is dammed up on the interior side of the Coast Mountains. The cold arctic air is very stable and heavy so it does not simply wash over the Coast Mountains but is forced to move through the valleys and inlets that pierce the mountain chain. The inlets that have the lowest connecting passes to the interior will be the first ones to receive the cold arctic air. As the depth of cold air continues to build over the interior the cold air will pour across higher passes and into other coastal inlets that didn't initially get the winds. The temperatures in the interior typically fall below -20°C during this period and values to -40°C are not uncommon.

Strong winds funnel down mainland inlets at speeds of up to 60 knots, and occasionally as high as 100 knots. Side tributaries from the main inlets can also have strong winds, and where a major side valley joins the main inlet chaotic conditions are found. Outflow winds are strongest within the confines of the inlet but ease and fan out when they flow outside the mouth. If the air coming out of the inlets is much colder, and as a result more dense than the air over the open water, then the outflow will extend as a plume some distance beyond the inlet opening. Areas just outside this plume will have little or no wind. Extreme caution is advised when crossing coastal inlets during an outflow event for winds can increase from light to gale or storm force almost instantly. It is like hitting a wall.

The exact direction of the northerly outflow winds varies across the coast depending on the local topography. In most cases the orientation of the mainland inlets is such that the winds are from the north or northeast but in some cases, such as Knight Inlet, the channel turns near its mouth so that the winds become easterly as they pass into Queen Charlotte Strait. The plume of winds that leaves the confines of the inlet is turned slightly by the prevailing winds over the open waters.

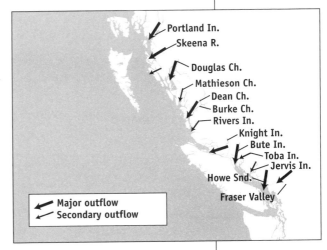

Portland In.
Skeena R.
Douglas Ch.
Mathieson Ch.
Dean Ch.
Burke Ch.
Rivers In.
Knight In.
Bute In.
Toba In.
Jervis In.
Howe Snd.
Fraser Valley

◀ Major outflow
◀ Secondary outflow

Because of the localized character of outflow winds, many weather observing stations do not experience them. The coastal stations that do give good indications of outflow are: Grey Islet and Green Island for Portland Inlet, Holland Rock for the Skeena R., Nanakwa Shoal buoy for Douglas Ch., and Cathedral Point for Bute Inlet and Dean Ch. Pulteney Pt. gives only a hint of the outflow from Knight Inlet. There are no reporting sites that observe Bute or Jervis outflow winds. Pam Rocks is a good indicator for Howe Sound outflow.

Climate records suggest that the first hint of cold northerly outflow winds occurs in mid-October. This is followed by a stronger event in mid-November, but the main shift toward cold northerly outflow winds begins in mid-to late December, and continues into early spring. In some years the worst cases of arctic outflow occur in February and March. Once an arctic outflow event begins it generally persists without respite for several days.

Traditionally January is the coldest month of the year, but in recent years, with water temperatures being higher, February has been colder. With outflow conditions in February it can be beautiful with sunshine and little rain.

The third type of northerly wind is a drainage wind created by cold air flowing down the mountains and into the inlets. Drainage winds are most prevalent in the spring and early summer when the snow persists on the mountaintops but the valleys are warm. They will be discussed in the section on summer diurnal westerlies. The map shows the main and secondary routes of outflow. The larger arrows mark the inlets that get the first and the strongest outflow winds. The smaller arrows show the tracks of the lesser, and later outflow.

Clouds and weather

The weather is generally clear with outflow conditions, for the air from the interior is much drier than that on the coast. The fact that the winds come down from the higher passes also adds a subsidence factor to clear whatever low clouds are present. Outflow conditions tend to be cold in winter because of the introduction of cold air from the interior, but also because under clear skies at night the temperature will drop. In summer, however, they tend to be warmer, simply because the clear air allows the sun to shine and to warm up the air.

With the first burst of true arctic air, the temperature in the coastal inlets can drop from 10°C to -10°C in a few hours.

The arctic front forms the leading edge of the cold air. Its arrival is the first indication of the deteriorating conditions to follow. The weather preceding the front gives little sign of impending changes. The barometer is often steady and the weather may seem quite settled. When the arctic front arrives, it is usually accompanied by snow flurries. As the front passes, the temperature drops sharply, the barometric pressure rises rapidly, and strong northerly outflow winds begin. The band of snow moves westward with the front, and as drier air moves into the area, flurries end, and skies clear. Clear skies will persist along the mainland coast throughout the period of outflow winds. The outflow conditions prevent frontal systems from drawing too near. With the first burst of true arctic air, the temperature can drop from 10°C to -10°C in a few hours. Temperatures at the head of the inlets may drop as low as -25°C.

As the cold air moves over the warmer waters of Dixon Entrance, Hecate Strait, and Queen Charlotte Sound, it will gradually pick up moisture so that when it encounters land, such as the Queen Charlotte Islands, it will form cloud as it rises up over the islands. This is the pattern that gives the east coast of the Queen Charlotte Islands much of its snowfall. A similar pattern sets up along the east side of Vancouver Island. When the interior ridge weakens a little, or moves eastward enough, then weather systems from the Pacific will move closer to the mainland coast and bring with them warmer, moisture-laden air. As this moist air arrives it first overrides the arctic air, and precipitation passing through it falls in the form of snow. Then, normally the approaching air quickly replaces the cold arctic air allowing the snow to change to rain. If the approaching system only brushes the coast and does not replace the cold air, then the snowfall could continue until the front passes and skies clear once more. Some of the heaviest snowfalls occur in this transition from cold to warmer air.

When the warm air pushes onto the mainland coast it will often ride up over the cold air that remains trapped at the heads of the inlets. As this happens the rain falling out of the clouds changes to freezing rain or ice pellets as it passes through the cold air of the inlets. This will continue either until the cold air is warmed by the advancing warmer air, or until the moisture-laden air moves off and allows the cold dry air to dominate once again.

The end of an arctic outbreak occurs when the cold air is forced away from the coast by the arrival of a Pacific storm. Unfortunately, this may be accompanied by even more unfavourable weather. As the storm approaches it brings warmer air from the Pacific. The precipitation with the associated front would be either rain, or mixed rain and snow. Some cold air may remain trapped in the inlets and is not immediately warmed up. The northerly winds through the inlets gradually ease as the southeast winds ahead of the front strengthen. Often, rain will be reported at the mouth of the inlets while snow continues farther up the inlet. Freezing rain can also occur in the inlets until the cold air is fully scoured out by the approaching warmer air. Freezing rain, or mixed rain and snow, can significantly reduce a vessel's radar efficiency.

Freezing spray

The strong northerly arctic outflow that races through the inlets creates extensive choppy waves, and blows spray off the top of the waves. The temperature of the air is so cold that once the spray is lifted into the air it is cooled below freezing, but doesn't solidify into ice until it makes contact with a boat, or some other obstacle. The icing will continue to build an ever-thickening layer, as long as the cold winds continue. This may cause a boat to lose its stability. One mariner suggested, "if you happen to get caught in freezing spray and cannot quickly get out of it, then turn tail and run with the wind, as the spray will be less."

> The marine forecast includes warnings of freezing spray when the winds and air temperatures are such that "severe" freezing spray is expected. A graph in the appendix shows the wind speeds and air temperatures that are required to create light, moderate and severe freezing spray.

Northerly outflow winds occur whenever the pressure-slope is in the northeastern half of the compass.

Seas

Most northerly winds pass through the coastal inlets before they spill out into the open, and as a result, the fetch of the winds is normally quite small. Since the winds decrease once they exit from the inlets, the seas that develop are not normally very large. But having said that, it should be remembered that the winds coming out of the inlets are in fanning plumes so there will be bands of higher seas where the winds are strong, and areas where they are considerably lower.

> The outflow event that created havoc in the Victoria area in December 1996 also created problems along the central coast. The temperature at Cathedral Point dropped below freezing on 20 December, and didn't rise above freezing again until the evening of 1 January 1997. The winds at Cathedral Pt. rose above gale force on 20 December and continued with gale force strength through the next eight days. The highest "mean" wind of 65 knots occurred on 22 December, and was the highest ever recorded at Cathedral Pt. On the ninth day the wind equipment finally stopped recording. The dock at Shearwater was torn up by the winds, and some of the boats (including the *Kabirian*) that were tied up there almost sank under one foot of ice from freezing spray.

Pressure-slope indications

In coastal inlets, northerly outflow winds occur whenever the pressure-slope is in the northeastern half of the compass, from about 300° to 130°. The regular, relatively light, northerly winds that occur when southeast winds are blowing in the open waters occur in the range of easterly pressure-slope, from 060° to 130°. But the strongest northerly outflow winds develop when the pressure-slope is between 340° and 060°. Winds in the remainder of the range from 300° to 340° remain as northerlies, but are generally quite light, and can be more variable in direction.

The winds in the inlets, being confined by the direction of the channels, are from the north or northeast, but outside the inlets, things are somewhat different. The winds after they leave the inlets are steered according to the pressure-slopes that are found farther to the west. The topography of the Queen Charlotte Islands and Vancouver Island also affects the wind directions, and as a result, the winds through the inner waters may become more easterly.

> One mariner suggested listening to the reports from the Alaska Panhandle to see if northerly winds might be expected to come out from the panhandle. However, winds that affect the waters above Sitka do not make it all the way down to Dixon Entrance.

The first example for 21/22 March 2002 clearly shows the plumes of stronger winds out of the inlets. The pressure-slope is near 040°. Note also the areas of lighter winds between the plumes. Lucy Island is generally in a wind shadow, but Holland Rock can get outflow from the Skeena River. Bonilla Island is in a wind shadow until the flow turns more northerly.

The easterly winds through Dixon Entrance appear to increase toward the west, but remembering that the images are showing surface roughness, what has actually been shown is that the seas gradually build as the fetch increases. The winds may actually decrease slightly through this distance. But what it clearly illustrates is that the direction of the winds remains due easterly. Easterly winds also pass out of the inlets on the west coasts of the Queen Charlotte Islands and Vancouver Island. Stronger winds and higher seas closer to the low are also shown to the southwest of Moresby Island.

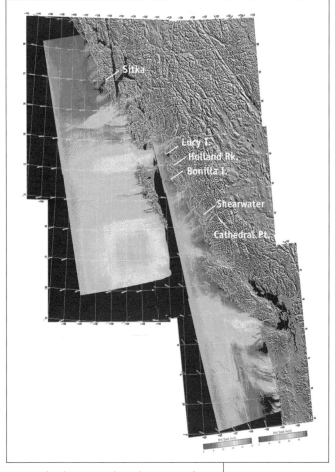

21/22 March 2002

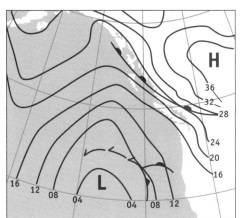

Note that the weather map shows that there is a low and front well to the southwest of the Charlottes. The satellite picture shows the cloud associated with the front, while the north coast remains perfectly clear.

81

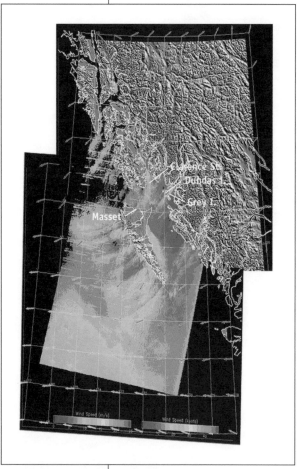

15 April 2001

The radar wind image for 15 April 2001 illustrates the pattern when the pressure-slope turns more toward the north. Now instead of the winds coming only out of Portland Inlet and streaming westward across Dixon Entrance, some winds move down through the channels of the Alaska Panhandle. The flow over Dixon Entrance, Hecate Strait, and out the inlets of the Charlottes is slightly more northerly when compared to the previous example. You can also notice that the plumes of winds bend once they exit the inlets. This is most noticeable just outside Clarence Strait. The radar wind images also indicate which mainland inlets have the strongest outflow.

During a true arctic outflow event the temperature at Grey Islet, just outside Portland Inlet, would fall to -5°C to -10°C, but in these spring examples the temperature was between 2°C and 4°C. Colder air would give more intense plumes of winds out of the inlets.

The only cloud on the coast is associated with the front well offshore. With a strong high over the interior the front would weaken offshore and only a few bands of cirrus might cross the coast.

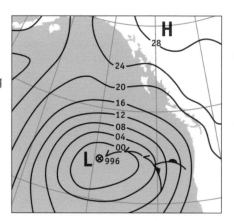

The northerly flow through the inlets will bend and turn following the direction of the inlet. The wind will flow around bends in the same way that water courses along a river. The winds will first be stronger on one side then will oscillate over to the other, but this will also change over time. When the outflow is fully underway most mariners think it is not safe to be in the inlets at all, even if you have local knowledge of where the relatively lighter winds will be.

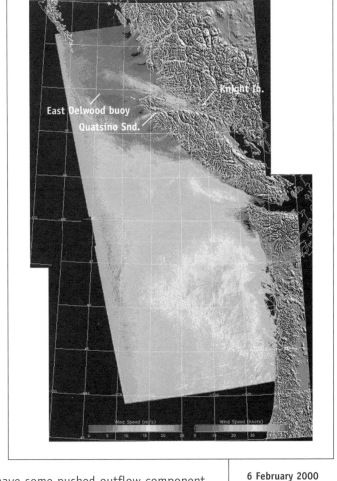

The paths of outflow over the south and central coasts are shown in this radar image for 6 February 2000. The pressure-slope in this case is near 030°. The outflow from Knight Inlet moves westward and extends out well beyond Queen Charlotte Strait. Some of this flow also passes through Quatsino Sound, and a lesser amount moves through a gap in the topography just south of Cape Scott. A plume of winds exiting from Juan de Fuca Strait would have some pushed outflow component from Howe Sound and the Fraser Valley, but is primarily drawn outward by the low to the south of Vancouver Island. Note the other inlets on Vancouver Island that have outflow winds, and the areas of lighter winds between them.

6 February 2000

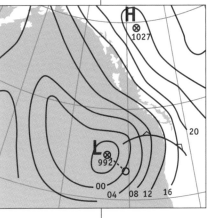

It has been said that if winds at Grey Islet are northeast 35 to 40 knots, Masset would be east to northeast 20 to 25 knots. In this example the seas would build through the 70 mile fetch from Dundas Island to Langara to about 3 to 4 metres. If the winds at Grey Islet were 50 to 60 knots, the seas off Langara would reach 5 to 6 metres. The seas remain lower near the mainland coast.

January wind roses

Southeast winds remain the dominant direction through the open waters though northerly winds are much stronger than they were in October. North to northeast winds are the dominant wind through the inlets of the mainland coast and Vancouver Island. In Dixon Entrance the dominant wind is easterly, and ranges from northeast to southeast. West of the Queen Charlotte Islands the dominant wind ranges between south and east. Through the inner waters the winds are predominantly southeast but also have significant northwest winds. In the Strait of Georgia and Juan de Fuca Strait the winds are almost polarized between northwest and southeast, or between west and east. Farther offshore the winds become more uniform, with little directional preference. This is clearly seen in the East Delwood buoy west of the Scott Islands.

Wind direction frequency

0-5
5-10
10-15
15-20
20-25
25-30
30-40
40-50
50-70
70-100

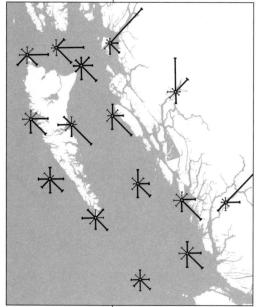

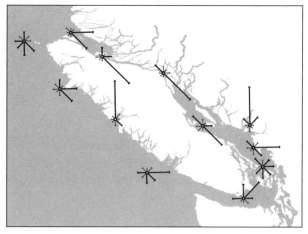

SOUTHERLY WINDS

Southerly winds are transitional winds. While they are not a frequently observed wind they are most common during the in-between times of the year, near the spring and fall equinoxes. They often follow a quiet period of nice weather in late February and early March. They generally occur after the passage of a front, as the winds shift from southeast to west. The winds normally decrease sharply behind the front so in most cases they are light and not a problem. In some situations, however, such as when a low crosses directly over the coast, the pressures may rise rapidly behind the front to produce very strong winds that are potentially dangerous. The dangerous aspect of southerly winds lies in the fact that in many places, docks, moorings, houses, and trees are not prepared for strong winds from this direction.

Southerly winds are most common during the in-between times of the year, near the spring and fall equinoxes.

The intensity of the southwest winds depends on the intensity of the front and the rate of pressure rises. The stronger the front is, the stronger are the winds. On the plus side, they are usually very brief. One mariner summed this up by saying, "southwest winds raise hell, but don't last long."

Clouds and weather

In the transition seasons of spring and early autumn, while all types of weather can be expected, none tends to last long. The typical pattern is to see the dark, overcast, rainy weather that occurs ahead of the front clear momentarily with its passage. Cumulus clouds soon arrive, or develop, behind the front, and showers spread across the region. If the temperature drops dramatically behind the front then the winds will be gusty, and the showers may be heavy and accompanied by thunder and hail. Waterspouts may also be observed in inlets and near headlands.

This southerly wind pattern can also develop when a weak ridge forms across the coast to the south of your area. When this happens clouds may be created over the local topography. Cumulus clouds form over the mountaintops, and patches of fog or stratus linger in the inlets.

Ocean Falls, situated about 100 miles north of Port Hardy, and 50 miles west of Bella Coola, was the largest community in the Central Coast in the 1950s when the paper mill was most active. Now with the mill closed it has a population of about 150 people year-round, but expands dramatically in the summer.

Seas

The seas also go through a change as the winds shift from one direction to another. Southeast seas may continue in the form of swell after the southeast winds end, and south to southwest wind waves begin to develop. The southerly wind waves will only be a problem if the winds are particularly strong. Southwest swells arrive after the passage of the front and affect those areas open to the west.

Pressure-slope indications

The typical pressure-slopes for southerly winds are between 130° and 200°. When the pressure-slope is near 130°, southeast winds may still be lingering in parts of the region. This is

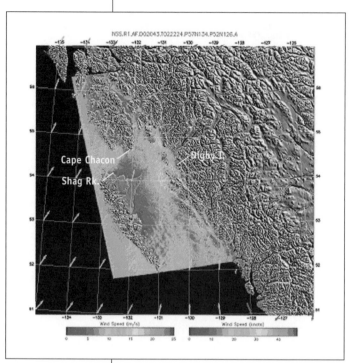

12 February 2002

in fact the case in the example of 12 February 2002 that has a pressure-slope of 130°. A warm front was over eastern Hecate Strait, and strong southeast winds were occurring throughout the channels of the mainland coast. The winds at Grey Islet, Holland Rock, and Lucy Island were between 33 and 38 knots. Bonilla's winds were only 22 knots, but Sandspit, on the Charlottes, had southerly winds of six knots. Note the strong winds that appear as waves over southern Moresby Island and southern Hecate Strait. Strong southwest winds spread along the west side of the Charlottes and over the corner of Graham Island into Dixon Entrance. With southeast winds still at Rose Spit the winds appear to converge a little west of Cape Chacon. Mariners have commented that Shag Rock is often the separation point along Graham Island between the westerlies and easterlies.

If the pressure-slope turns toward the south, the winds veer toward the west. The winds cross the Charlottes leaving bands of lighter winds that extend downwind from the larger mountains. In some cases when cold air spreads in behind the front the air is unstable and the winds as a result are gusty. Ice pellets, hail, and thunder may accompany these gusty winds.

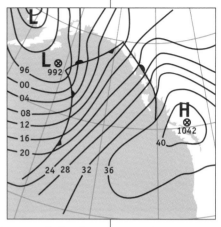

12 February 2002

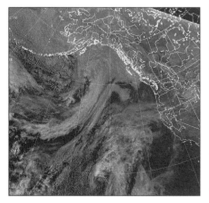

The weather map for two hours before the radar wind image shows the warm front along the mainland coast. A sizeable area of cloud associated with the front covers the north coast. The cold front extends to the southwest of the low, which lies near the bent-back hook some 600 nautical miles west of the Queen Charlotte Islands.

In this south coast example of 12 March 2002, the main low was moving toward the Queen Charlotte Islands, and the associated front had just crossed the south coast. The pressure-slope was near 150° over Vancouver Island. Winds spread directly onto the west coast of Vancouver Island and entered all the inlets.

These winds were noticeably stronger than the winds through the Strait of Georgia. A band of strong winds moved northward from Juan de Fuca Strait across the San Juan Islands.

12 March 2002
→

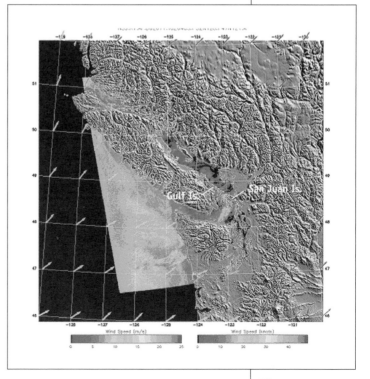

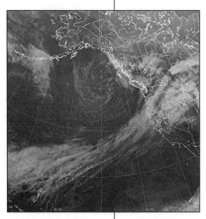

12 March 2002

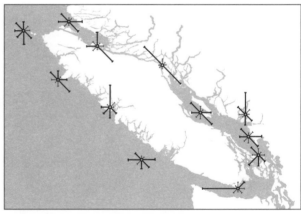

Strong southerly winds also spread through Queen Charlotte Strait, and were strongest along the northern shoreline.

The satellite image shows the front, marked by the long band of cloud stretching southwest from Oregon. Another trough rotating around the low lies over the north coast.

April wind roses

Wind direction frequency

0-5	-
5-10	—
10-15	⊢
15-20	⊢
20-25	⊢
25-30	⊢
30-40	⊢—
40-50	⊢—
50-70	⊢——
70-100	⊢————

The dominant wind in Hecate Strait continues to be from the southeast but now the winds from the northwest are becoming a little more noticeable. Winds in Dixon Entrance are still mainly from the east and southeast, though the frequency of westerly winds has increased since January. The major change is through the inlets where the south and southwest winds are now almost as frequent as the north-easterlies. The shift in regimes has begun,

from the winter outflow to the summer inflow. The winds west of the Charlottes have an almost even spread of wind directions. The winds have little directional preference in April. Most locations show more westerly winds than in January but still have dominant easterly winds. Outflow winds still prevail through the inlets of the mainland coast and Vancouver Island.

WESTERLY WINDS

Westerly winds develop in one of three different ways. The first is when a ridge builds behind a passing front. The strength of the ridge will vary depending on whether a deep low remains to the northwest of the region after the front has passed. If it does, the pressures do not rise significantly until after a secondary trough passes over the area. The strongest westerly winds occur when the pressures rise very rapidly after the passage of the front. These are **post-frontal westerly** *winds.*

The strongest westerly winds occur when the pressures rise very rapidly after the passage of the front.

The second pattern for westerly winds develops when a ridge builds northward from the sub-tropical high. This is most common during the months from April through September. The orientation of the ridge dictates where the strongest winds will occur, just like the orientation of the front changed the location of the strongest easterly winds. The difference, however, is not as pronounced as with easterlies, for the winds are generally not as strong. These are **offshore-ridge westerly** winds.

The third type of westerly wind develops due to strong daytime heating in the summer, and as a result, is called a **diurnal westerly** wind. Diurnal winds are caused through an imbalance in temperature between two places. When the temperature rises in one place more than another, the pressure in the higher temperature area will fall a little more than in the other, creating a pressure difference between the two. Winds will start to blow from the higher to lower pressure. These winds are, from one point of view, the same as any other wind in that they blow from higher to lower pressure, but they differ in the root cause of the pressure difference.

> The word diurnal comes from the Latin noun "dies," which means "day," and from "diurnalis" meaning "daily." In weather usage, the word diurnal refers to changes that take place in weather elements, such as wind, pressure or temperature, because of the heating and cooling patterns of the day.

Westerly winds that develop after the passage of a front generally rise rapidly, but only last a matter of hours before the next front approaches. While they may be short lived, they can at times be very strong, especially if the pressure rises very rapidly. This impact is worse when the air is cold and has more "bite." One of the biggest concerns arises from the rapid change in wind direction. What was a safe anchorage for southeast winds (such as McIntyre Bay, west of Rose Spit) may provide no protection from westerly winds.

The offshore-ridge westerlies, on the other hand, tend to last for days, not hours. Their duration and strength depends on the orientation and position of the ridge. The north coast is almost at the most northerly end of the ridge from the sub-tropical high so only a small change results in the ridge moving south of the area. Consequently, frontal troughs from the Gulf of Alaska are able to affect the region. What often happens is that the ridge will build strongly north for a few days, then will weaken and rotate over Queen Charlotte Sound. To the north of the ridge the winds will back into the south as frontal troughs approach the area, while northwest winds continue over waters farther to the south. The ridge may later build northward again and repeat the pattern.

> The period from mid-July to mid-August is the time when the ridge is normally strongest and farthest north. But soon after, the ridge begins to weaken as the sub-tropical high starts moving southward. This is shown by the fact that the chance of precipitation increases in the far north after late July and more noticeably after mid-August.

Diurnal winds are a localized phenomenon that occurs when the sun is strong enough to cause these slight pressure differences. Through most of the year these subtle pressure differences are overshadowed by the bigger scale dynamic pressure changes of the passing weather systems. A diurnal wind can be from any direction, for it only depends on where the temperature is higher. Land and sea breezes are specific types of diurnal winds, and their direction is solely tied to the orientation of the land-ocean edge at a specific location.

Diurnal winds are so connected to the strength of daytime heating that they are easily influenced by a number of things, such as the passage of a little cloud overhead, or the thickness of morning fog that restricts the hours of sunshine. Both post-frontal and offshore-ridge winds can be estimated by the gradient on weather maps, but diurnal winds are often so local in nature, that they will not be seen on weather maps. Diurnal westerly winds do have a typical cycle of being light overnight, rising around 10 or 11 in the morning, reaching their peak in the late afternoon or evening, then dropping quickly to light again just before sunset. In some areas, such as in the Strait of Georgia, the diurnal winds do not have the same timing, for they are the result of the diurnal cycle from elsewhere, in this example from farther upstream in Queen Charlotte Strait.

A diurnal wind can be from any direction, for it only depends on where the temperature is higher.

As part of the diurnal cycle of a summer day, the sides of the inlets heat up and air is drawn up the inlets as inflow winds. At night the air cools over the mountaintops and drains down through the inlets. Sometimes these northerly outflow winds can come suddenly, as if a dam was broken.

Some areas will have stronger winds when the flow is more westerly than when it is northwesterly, while for other areas it will be the opposite. Likewise some areas will get lee sheltering in certain wind directions but not in others. It may take a very small change in wind direction to make the difference. Vancouver Island provides a noticeable lee shelter for the southwestern part of the island when the winds are almost northerly, and for Queen Charlotte and Johnstone straits when the winds are more southerly. The flow over the Queen Charlotte Islands is similar, but since the mountains are lower than on Vancouver Island, and since Moresby Island becomes quite narrow in the south, the topographical effects are somewhat weaker.

Clouds and weather

A westerly flow normally clears the solid overcast skies and continuous rain that occurs with an easterly pressure-slope, and replaces it with a mix of sun and cloud, and the occasional shower. The ridge of high pressure, having sub-siding air, prevents the development of any large areas of mid and high level clouds. If a weak frontal system passes over the ridge, then some amounts of cirrus may appear, either of the filament type, or as a veil of cirrostratus. Sometimes the veil thickens and changes to altostratus. At other times shields of altocumulus will pass across the region, with little or no cirrus above, and no cloud beneath it.

Westerly winds that arise after the passage of a front are often associated with colder, more unstable air, so they may be accompanied by large cumulus and cumulonimbus buildups and showers, which can be heavy with thunder and hail.

Fog

Since the pattern of westerly winds tends to occur in the summer half of the year, the subtle differences in temperature from place to place play a large role in the weather. Whenever warm moist air flows over colder water, fog develops. This fog may, depending on the strength of winds, be lifted slightly above the surface to form a layer of stratus clouds. The presence of fog, and its diurnal formation and dissipation cycles, is common during the period of westerlies. Fog is most common in the southwest corner of Queen Charlotte Sound, and off southwestern Vancouver Island, in the late summer and early autumn. August has been called "Fogust" by some mariners.

> The Prince Rupert area will generally get fog after two or three days of sun, and once it has formed, it takes longer and longer each day to lift. It rolls back in from the south, over Digby Island during the evening, around 1830 to 1930 hours.

Fog is another summer phenomenon that is strongly connected with diurnal winds. Fog and diurnal winds are as connected as two sides of the same coin. Fog forms after the winds ease. Winds develop after the fog dissipates. When the fog is present the air is not heated. When the winds are strong the fog doesn't form. Each influences the other; both are linked to daytime heating, and will form earlier or later, depending on the strength of the heating. As the winds pick up, the fog starts to lift.

Seas

The seas in a westerly flow can be considerably higher in the open western waters than in the more sheltered inside waters. The wind fetch with westerly winds is basically unlimited outside the islands. The duration of the wind is also greater with ridges, for they tend to be slower moving than fronts. As a result, the seas associated with westerly winds are primarily controlled by just the wind speed. Higher winds create higher seas. In the inner waters, however, fetch limits the height of seas for all wind speeds.

Swells can arrive onto the coast, no matter what direction the local winds. The swells themselves, however, are a threat to the outer coast when they develop in the westerly winds around some distant storm, and as a result, generally come from a westerly direction. They tend to move at speeds of 30 to 40 knots, so can move from the offshore buoys to the coast in a matter of a few hours. Heights of 10 to 12 metres are possible along the west side of the Queen Charlotte Islands. The swells that move toward Vancouver Island are usually somewhat lower.

Pressure-slope indications

Post-frontal and offshore-ridge westerlies are strongly influenced by the orientation of the pressure-slope, while diurnal winds are much less so. The general pressure-slope domain of westerlies is between 200° and 300°. Within this range winds vary between west and northwest, but in many instances the variations from west to northwest are more influenced by topography than by slight shifts of pressure-slope. Winds in some areas will blow from due west throughout this pressure-slope range, while other locations remain from the northwest. Where the topography allows, however, the tendency would be that the winds are westerly when the pressure-slope is near 200°, and northwesterly when it tilts toward 300°. The following three radar wind images show most variations that occur within the realm of westerly winds.

The first example of 20 September 2002 occurred just after the passage of a front, which is seen on the satellite picture over Washington State. The pressure-slope had just turned from 170° ahead of the front to near 240° behind it.

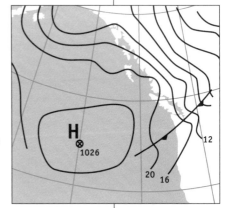

20 September 2002

This radar image can be compared to the one for 12 March 2002, shown in the section on southerly winds, which had a pressure-slope near 150°. The westerly winds in both cases impact the entire length of the west coast of Vancouver Island, but in this September case the winds run more parallel with the island and only spread a short distance into some of the inlets.

20 September 2002

➜

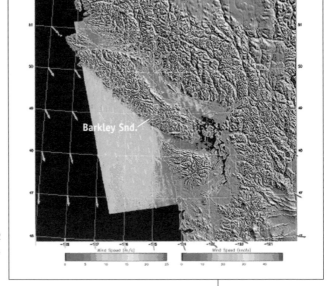

the four winds

The westerly winds in Juan de Fuca Strait, which turned north across the San Juan Islands in the 12 March case, now continue toward the east without turning north. The northwest winds in the Strait of Georgia also continued toward the Fraser Valley, and as a result, left the Gulf and San Juan Islands in a near calm wind shadow. The winds in the Strait of Georgia appeared to move in waves, with bands of strong and weaker winds. These bands, which resemble waves on a beach and the pattern of some clouds, formed in the colder, unstable air behind the front. The westerly winds in Queen Charlotte Strait are not noticeably stronger on the northern shoreline but increase over eastern sections and in Johnstone Strait.

**0800 hours
15 August 2002**

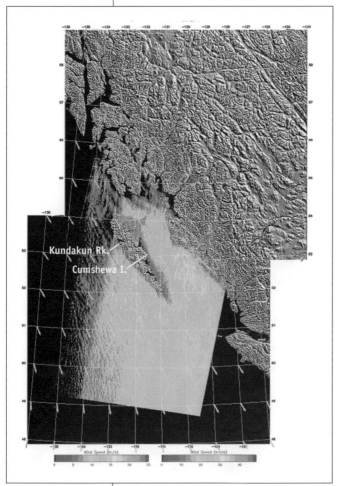

The second radar wind image is for 0800 hours on 15 August 2002. The pressure-slope at that time was near 280°. Northerly winds that moved out from the channels of the southern Alaska Panhandle ran down the full length of Hecate Strait. Areas of lee sheltering can be seen immediately adjacent to the east side of the Queen Charlotte Islands, and over the west side of Graham Island. The winds continue to blow down the west side of Moresby Island. The northwest winds spread into some of the channels along the east side of Hecate Strait, with lee sheltering downwind of some of the islands. The location of these wind shadows shifts with very small changes in the pressure-slope, and the associated winds. Mariners listen to the reports from Kindakun Rock and Cumshewa Island to determine on which side of the Queen Charlotte Islands the wind is blowing.

The weather map has a ridge of high pressure offshore. A weak lee trough occurs over southwest Vancouver Island.

Apart from some cirrus west of the Charlottes the only cloud is a finger of fog and stratus along the Washington coast and off the mouth of Juan de Fuca Strait.

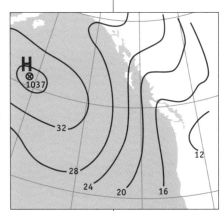

0800 hours →
15 August 2002

←

The third radar image, which has a pressure-slope near 260°, was taken at 1900 hours on 15 August 2002. A plume of strong northwest winds extended south from northern Vancouver Island. The winds were light to the southeast of this plume and likely were from the east or northeast. Lee sheltering also occurred downwind of various islands and peninsulas, such as the area immediately southeast of the Brooks Peninsula. The westerly winds increased in

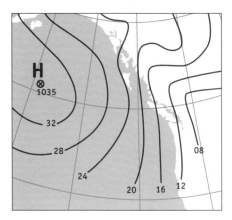

1900 hours
15 August 2002

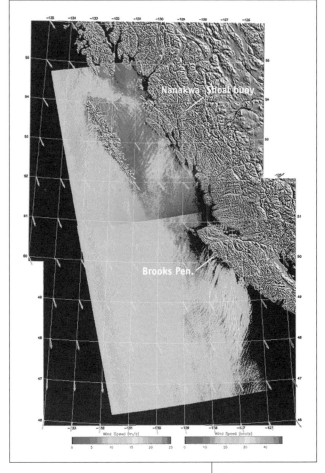

strength in Queen Charlotte Strait. The winds that spread down the full length of west Vancouver Island in the 20 September example, are now seen in this August example to lie farther off the southern part of the island, since the pressure-slope rotated from southwest to near west. In the summer, with heating along the coast, there is a tendency for the offshore plume of winds to collapse onto the coast during the afternoon, then move offshore again overnight. These diurnal changes are not always shown on weather maps.

Westerly winds spread through Dixon Entrance and across to the mainland coast south of Prince Rupert. Northwest winds run down the west coast of the Queen Charlotte Islands and pass over western Queen Charlotte Sound, but do not extend eastward into the sound. A wedge-shaped area of lighter winds has formed in the lee of the Queen Charlotte Islands, but the northwest winds increased again over the southeastern parts of Hecate Strait. Another area of lighter winds occurred over the mainland coast, close to Vancouver Island, and spread all around the top of the island. This area of lighter winds is likely due to lee sheltering from the mainland coast.

**1900 hours
15 August 2002**

The two radar images on 15 August 2002 show some interesting aspects of the diurnal wind pattern. The first thing to note is that the pressure-slope backed about 10 to 20 degrees during the course of the day, as it shifted from north of west, to just south of west. The strong winds that spread through the length of Hecate Strait in the morning eased close to the Queen Charlotte Islands during the afternoon as the winds turned enough to create the area of lee sheltering. If the ridge maintains the same position and strength the cycle would repeat, with the area of lee sheltering collapsing as the winds turn back into the northwest overnight.

The only change in the satellite image from the one for earlier in the day is the clearing of some of the fog off Juan de Fuca Strait.

July wind roses

July sees west and northwest winds as the dominant wind for all offshore coastal areas. The open areas west of the Queen Charlotte Islands and Vancouver Island, and in Hecate Strait and Queen Charlotte Sound, all have northwest winds. Dixon Entrance, Queen Charlotte Strait, and Juan de Fuca Strait have westerly winds. The inlets have inflow winds that are parallel with their channels. The Nanakwa Shoal buoy in Douglas Channel is located close to the junction of two channels, and hence has two main winds, one aligned with each channel.

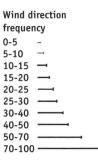

Wind direction
frequency

0-5	-
5-10	—
10-15	—
15-20	—
20-25	—
25-30	—
30-40	—
40-50	—
50-70	—
70-100	—

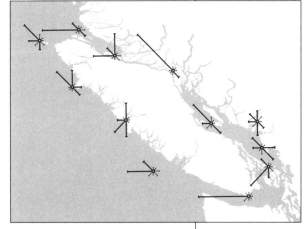

COASTAL LOWS

Coastal lows are potentially dangerous for three reasons. The first is that the strongest winds are normally close to the centre of the low, which in these cases passes right across the coast. The second is that the track of the low is critical, and is difficult to predict with precision. The third is that the low may begin to develop very close to the coast so the normal signs of development, such as thickening high clouds, may not appear until the low is right on top of you. If the low develops very rapidly, or to use a more dramatic term, explosively, then it is called a meteorological "bomb." This is the worst of all combinations, for if a low develops very rapidly (bombs) just off the coast, then the conditions will appear very benign until all of a sudden it becomes extremely nasty. Even if the forecast does give ample warning of its expected development, the mariner will have no visual confirmation that it is happening until it is too late. This appeared to have been the case with the storm of 26 October 2001 when the Kella-Lee sank northwest of Cape Scott, and two fishermen lost their lives.

> As there are such sharp variations in the strength of winds around the low it is important to be aware of the exact track of the low. A mariner who is south of the track of a coastal low would experience much worse conditions than north of the low.

With a rapidly deepening low that is moving quickly toward the coast, the pressure will fall rapidly ahead of the low with almost equal rises behind. In the case of the 26 October storm, the pressure fell ahead of the low at a rate of 15 millibars in three hours at Kindakun Rock. The pressure then rose 16 millibars in three hours behind it. Fortunately, not all coastal lows are this strong, but the potential is always there.

One of the most preferred tracks for a coastal low is over Queen Charlotte Sound and into southern Hecate Strait. If it turns northward soon enough it will sometimes travel the full length of Hecate Strait, passing just north of Prince Rupert, before it crosses the mainland Coast Mountains. If it tracks farther south, the preference seems to be to cross Barkley Sound, or to go through Juan de Fuca Strait.

19 March 2001

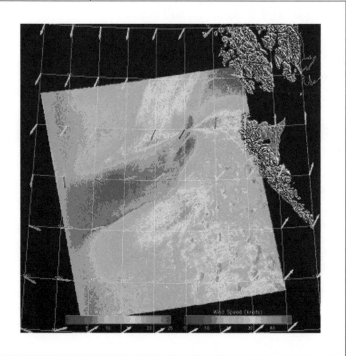

The radar example of 19 March 2001 has a low passing just northwest of the Queen Charlotte Islands. Around the low are pin-wheel bands of strong and weak winds. Strong easterly winds extending from Langara Island into the low are mirrored by the strong winds from the west-south-west. A band of lighter northeast winds are northeast of the low, with lighter southwest winds to the southwest.

Stronger winds also move toward the low from the north and south. These bands don't rotate around the low but translate

northeastward with it. The patchy cells indicate that the southwest winds are gusty due to unstable air.

The pattern of clouds and weather is basically the same as that with an approaching front. The

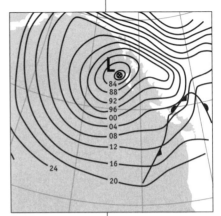

19 March 2001

only difference is that the entire cycle of clouds will take place, including the transition to cumulus and cumulonimbus clouds, which does not occur with every frontal passage. The visibility will be poor in rain and fog.

In this example of 19 March 2001 the highest seas only rose to just above 5 metres, but in more severe cases such as the 26 October 2001 storm when the *Kella-Lee* sank, and in the following case of 12 November 2002, the seas rose to 9 to 10 metres in the southeast winds ahead of the low, with seas of 10 to 12 metres with the south to southwest winds behind the low and associated front. The lowest seas, perhaps only building to 2 to 3 metres, would normally occur in the northeast quadrant ahead of the low. Mariners should always keep in mind that these wave reports, which were from the weather buoys, are the significant wave height values. The most extreme waves will occasionally rise to twice these significant wave height values.

0800 hours
12 November 2002

The last two radar wind images are not for a coastal low, for the featured low did not cross the BC coast, but tracked due north, passing so close to the Queen Charlotte Islands that it exhibited features of a coastal low. But these radar images are so marvellous, and so clearly show a number of features discussed earlier, that they must be shown. The two images were taken at 0800 and 1900 hours on 12 November 2002. After one of the driest Octobers on record for the southern BC coast, the weather pattern shifted dramatically. Instead of

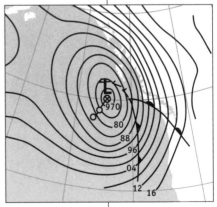

having a ridge of high pressure over the interior giving dry, but cool, outflow winds, the ridge moved farther east allowing a deep upper trough of low pressure to approach the coast. The 12 November storm was one of many that hit the coast after this shift.

In the morning of 12 November 2002 the low deepened as it moved from the southwest toward Vancouver Island. The low then tracked due north, passing just west of the Queen Charlotte Islands. The pressure-slope ahead of the low was from the northeast, near 040° over Dixon Entrance and near 060° over Hecate Strait.

0800 hours
12 November 2002

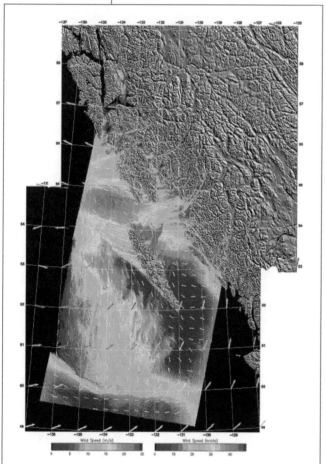

Northeast winds poured out of the inlets of the mainland coast and spread across Dixon Entrance ahead of the approaching front. The winds in Hecate Strait were from the southeast, but since the pressure-slope was from the northeast the strongest winds were close to the Queen Charlotte Islands and no southeast winds moved into the islands along the eastern strait. Southeast winds moved up both sides of the Queen Charlotte Islands, but the strong winds off Graham Island were primarily from the inlets with much reduced winds in between.

As the low tracked farther north the pressure-slope rotated into the southeast. When this shift occurred the northeast winds ended and southeast winds spread

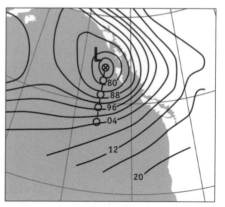

1900 hours
12 November 2002
→

right across eastern Dixon Entrance. Strong winds also poured through the channels of the eastern coastal edge of Hecate Strait. South of the low the pressure-slope shifted again into the south, and west to southwest winds spread across the southern Charlottes and into southern Hecate Strait. Southeast winds rose to storm force at a number of locations farther south and reached hurricane force off northwest Vancouver Island. Seas built to 10.3 metres at the South Hecate buoy at 1600 hours, just before the time of this second radar image. Cape St. James rose to southeast 53 knots, with gusts to 65 ahead of the low and front, and veered to southwest 46 knots gusting to 54 west of the front.

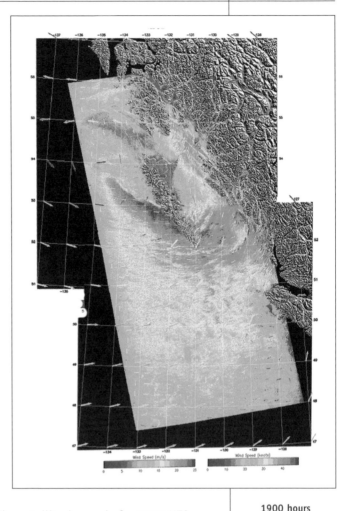

1900 hours
12 November 2002

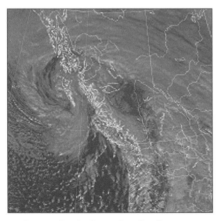

The satellite image is for 2100 UTC (1300 hours) 12 November 2002, partway between the times of the two radar images. It clearly shows the spiral arms of cloud around the low just west of the Charlottes. The area of cumulus and cumulonimbus clouds that accompanies the strong gusty southwest winds behind the front is seen moving onto Vancouver Island.

**The Western
(or Pacific) Yew is
found all across
the BC coast.
Its wood has had
many uses in the
past, ranging from
bows to lutes.
Today its bark is
known to contain
substances
effective against
some cancers.**

SUMMARY

It is hoped that this look at the five weather patterns, and the variations that can take place within each, will help the mariner realize that the weather experienced on the coast is something more than chaos. The changes of winds and weather are parts of patterns that can be recognized. The pressure-slope concept and the radar wind images are tools that can be used to increase the understanding of these patterns.

To see other radar wind images look at the internet site http://fermi.jhuapl.edu/sar/stormwatch/web_wind/ or do a search for Synthetic aperture radar wind images.

While the mariner experiences the winds increasing and decreasing in one spot, or over a range of locations if underway, the variations discussed here provide the bigger picture and cover the entire coast through the course of the year. This new perspective may be a challenge, but offers insights into the overall workings of the weather. The mariner will need to tailor the basic weather patterns with knowledge of local conditions. The next chapter introduces a number of local variations that can occur within each of the four wind directions.

regional weather guides

THE SOUTH COAST AND THE NORTH COAST

GENERAL WEATHER CONDITIONS

THIS CHAPTER is the fourth step toward finding a greater understanding of coastal weather.

The first step built a foundation based on an inner imagination of weather. The second looked at patterns and principles that apply to weather on our coast. The third step considered the various weather systems that affect the coast, and how they can be interpreted with the use of the pressure-slope concept. This fourth step is the most focussed of all, as it looks at the variations of winds, waves, and weather that occur through seven regions of the coast. A fifth and final step in this learning process is needed, but it is not found in this book, for it can only be taken by every person who wants to really understand the weather that they encounter. The final step requires taking whatever is found useful in this book, and in other books, making it your own, and building a working knowledge that can become a practical guide for "living with weather" along the BC coast.

It should be remembered that when one place is mentioned as having particularly strong winds or waves it does not mean that other places do not experience similar conditions. Observe how the winds and waves respond to geographical features in certain weather patterns, and then watch for similar conditions at other locations with similar features.

The little compass icon in the upper corner of each page indicates the wind direction that is under discussion. The northern quadrant of the compass, for example, is filled in when northerly winds are being considered.

Winds

The graph shows the pattern of winds through the course of the year. One line shows the frequency of gale force winds (34kts) or higher, averaged over eight coastal stations (Solander Island, Sartine Island, Bonilla Island, Rose Spit, Kindakun Rock, Sandspit, Herbert Island, and Egg Island). The second line shows the average winds for Herbert Island. While the two lines have different values (as shown on the two vertical axes) the peaks and troughs

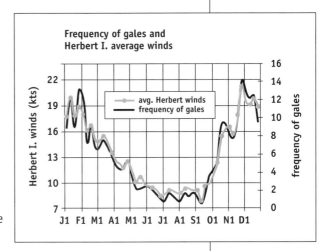

Frequency of gales and Herbert I. average winds

almost exactly match, which suggests that they are both responding to the same yearly rhythms of wind strength.

The exact direction of the flow of winds in any area varies with changes in the orientation of the isobars, which is indicated by the pressure-slope. Offshore all wind directions are possible, but within the confined waters of the inlets and the inner south coast, they tend to shift from one direction to another, with only light winds from any direction in between. The strength of winds around headlands and in inlets can change significantly with a 10 or 20 degree change in wind direction, or pressure-slope.

Waves

The wind waves that are generated within the inside coastal waters are significantly limited by the fetch distance. Graphs in the appendix show what wave heights develop for various wind speeds, fetch, and duration. Environment Canada's CD-ROM *Coastal Weather for British Columbia Mariners* has a calculator that calculates the wave heights for all wind speeds.

Precipitation

The total amount of rain or snow (the total precipitation) that falls over the region throughout the year is greatest where the winds blow directly onshore, and increases with height above the water. Since the prevailing flow is from the west, the western slopes of Vancouver Island, the Queen Charlotte Islands and the central coast get more rain than the areas on the east side of the islands, where subsidence provides a rain shadow.

> Why are there rain shadows on the east sides of Vancouver Island and the Queen Charlotte Islands when the dominant wind during the rainy winter period is from the southeast? One might think that the rain shadow should be on the west side of the islands. The reason for this seeming contradiction is that when the surface winds are southeast the winds above the surface are southwest, and it is these upper southwest winds that are responsible for the upslope effects and the increased precipitation on the west facing slopes.

The strong rain shadow effect downwind of the Olympic Mountains and the mountains of Vancouver Island allow Victoria, the Gulf Islands, and much of the inside waters around the Strait of Georgia to have the lowest annual precipitation on the coast. The eastern side of the Queen Charlotte Islands, particularly eastern Graham Island, and the inside waters of Vancouver Island from just west of Port McNeil to the southern parts of the Broughton

Archipelago, also have significantly less precipitation than surrounding areas.

The precipitation map below displays the variations of annual precipitation across the coast. It is based on data from regular reporting sites, plus many volunteer observations, but this still leaves many areas without measurements. A computer program has modelled the remaining locations to provide "best guess" values.

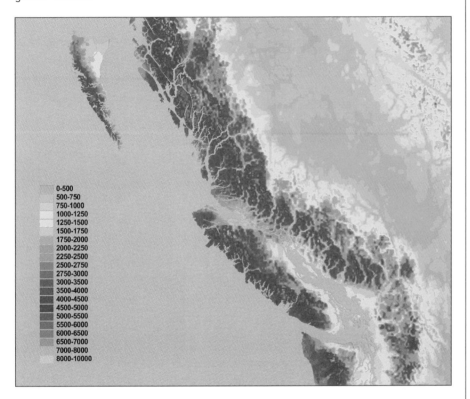

0-500
500-750
750-1000
1000-1250
1250-1500
1500-1750
1750-2000
2000-2250
2250-2500
2500-2750
2750-3000
3000-3500
3500-4000
4000-4500
4500-5000
5000-5500
5500-6000
6000-6500
6500-7000
7000-8000
8000-10000

Variations of annual precipitation across the coast.

←

How much rain falls over the open ocean? The exact answer is not known as rainfall is not measured over the ocean. Likely, it receives more than the areas that have lee sheltering but less than the high amounts of the mountainous areas. A best guess is that the average annual rainfall over the ocean is near 1400mm in the north, and 1000mm in the south.

The yearly pattern of precipitation, which falls mainly as rain, follows a pattern that is similar throughout the coast. In the autumn the rainfall increases fairly abruptly, and reaches a peak in late October. On average, there is a relative lull in the rainfall amounts in mid-November. This lull coincides with the first onset of northerly outflow winds. This is followed by a slight increase again in early December, and a sharp drop in late December. The rate of precipitation is twice as high as shown in the graph in the areas that receive the most precipitation, and half as high in the Georgia Basin, which receives much less precipitation. The pattern of precipitation changes, however, is similar all along the coast.

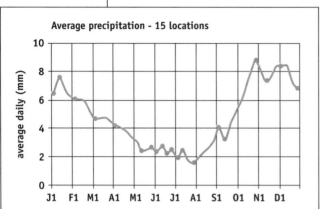

Temperature

The temperatures across the coast are closely related to the water temperature. In places such as Bella Coola, which are well removed from the open Pacific Ocean, the temperature takes on a more continental character, with hotter summers and colder winters. Air moving from the water over the land spreads cooler marine air a short distance inland during the summer, and spreads milder air inland in winter. The reverse is true when air moves from the land over the water, as the air over the land is hotter in the summer and cooler in winter.

The average minimum air temperatures in January during the thirty year period between 1970 and 2000 have risen by about one full degree Celsius compared to the thirty year period 1950 to 1980. The sea surface temperature at Pine Island has increased by one degree between the years 1950 and 2000. The maximum temperatures in August have not changed significantly. The precipitation over this period has increased slightly, while the warmer water temperatures have resulted in a reduction in the amount of fog.

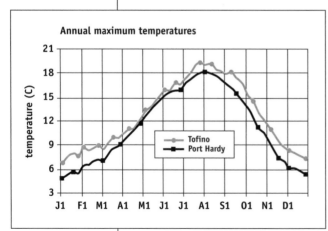

Fog

Visibility is reduced to some degree throughout the year in all varieties of precipitation. With heavy rain or drizzle the air becomes nearly saturated, and the visibility can drop below ½ mile, which is the definition of fog. Above this value it is officially called mist. Fog by itself, without the visibility restrictions of rain or drizzle, is primarily a local phenomenon that is caused when air is cooled enough to condense the water vapour in the air.

During the summer and early autumn, warm air is cooled from below when it passes over cold water. The colder the water, the more likely it will create fog. As a result the areas that are most fog prone are places where the waters tend to be cold, either due to cold currents or from upwelling of cold subsurface waters. Fog is most frequent from mid-July to mid-October, with the peak often being during the second week in August. In the cooler days of autumn "radiation" fog is more common during the early morning hours over land. The flatter lands of the Fraser Valley and the boggy lands of northeast Graham Island are both prime locations for this type of fog. The adjacent waters remain clear.

Stratus and fog near northern and southwestern Vancouver Island.

Sunshine

There is little difference in sunshine amounts across the coast from November through April, but there is quite a variation in July and August. All stations have a peak in May with a slight decline in June. For Prince Rupert and Sandspit this May peak is their yearly high, while elsewhere on the coast the maximum sunshine is in July.

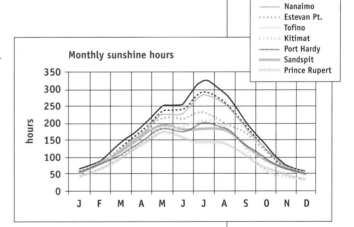

Monthly sunshine hours

Victoria
Vancouver
Nanaimo
Estevan Pt.
Tofino
Kitimat
Port Hardy
Sandspit
Prince Rupert

South Coast

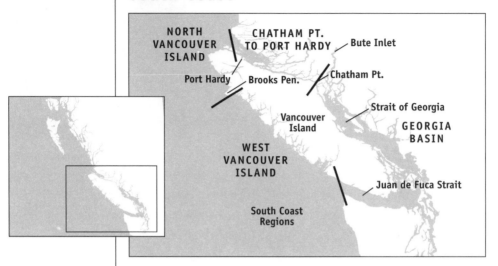

NORTH VANCOUVER ISLAND

CHATHAM PT. TO PORT HARDY — Bute Inlet

Port Hardy — Brooks Pen. — Chatham Pt.

Strait of Georgia

GEORGIA BASIN

Vancouver Island

WEST VANCOUVER ISLAND

Juan de Fuca Strait

South Coast Regions

The South Coast has been divided into two regions east of Vancouver Island, and two regions to the west. The inside water areas includes the area from **Chatham Point to Port Hardy**, *and the* **Georgia Basin**, *which stretches from Juan de Fuca Strait through the Strait of Georgia and include the inlets of the mainland coast. The two outside regions are:* **North Vancouver Island**, *which goes from Port Hardy to the Brooks Peninsula; and* **West Vancouver Island**, *which continues from just south of the Brooks Peninsula to the opening of Juan de Fuca Strait. The conditions in the Georgia Basin area are covered in more detail in the book,* The Wind Came All Ways.

Georgia Basin

The Georgia Basin has fascinatingly complicated winds. The winds may switch to westerly in some part of the region while remaining easterly in other parts, or vice versa. The summary below follows the idea used in *The Wind Came All Ways* of organizing the winds by pressure-slope rather than by wind direction. This organization provides a more complete understanding. The Georgia Basin is like a large bathtub in that the winds tend to slosh in one direction, and then turn, and move back in the other direction. The winds can be quite dynamic with one area increasing in strength, as another area is weakening. For this book some variations have been made to the original pressure-slope categories in order to group them into the four main winds.

EASTERLY PRESSURE-SLOPE WINDS

When a front moves south across Vancouver Island, the pressure-slope rotates toward the east and southeast. Winds are drawn up the Strait of Georgia from the southeast. Since the winds are strongest close to the front, and since the front weakens as it moves down over the Georgia Basin the winds are generally strongest in the northern part of the strait. Southeast winds that blow over the whole strait can build seas to three metres at the northern end with typical fronts, and up to five metres in the most extreme events. These winds are usually equally strong on both sides of the strait.

Southeast winds rise to strong to gale force at the west and east entrances of Juan de Fuca Strait but generally remain light easterly through the middle of the strait. In the strongest events a plume of strong southeast winds passes through Puget Sound, and then across the eastern end of the strait and through the San Juan Islands. Haro Strait will be particularly strong. This plume of southeast winds at the eastern entrance may form a distinct band that presents a formidable wall of winds when travelling from the west. The edge of the winds generally does not extend east of the line from Dungeness Spit to Albert Head, just west of Victoria. In

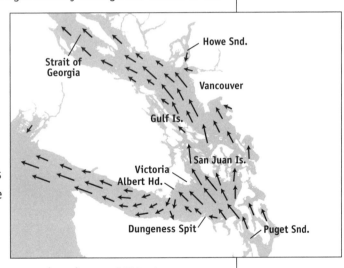

unusual and brief occasions, when the pressure-slope is near 080°, stronger easterly winds will spread throughout the entire length of the strait.

"I begin to see that everything is perfectly balanced, that everything has its own place, but is interdependent on the rest, that a picture, like life, must also have perfect balance. Every part of it also is dependent on the whole and the whole is dependent on every part...Oh to be still enough to hear and see and know the glory of the sky and earth and sea."

EMILY CARR FROM HER JOURNALS

NORTHERLY PRESSURE-SLOPE WINDS

When the pressure-slope is near 060° winds blow from the northwest in the northern part of the Strait of Georgia and from the southeast in the south. The

northwest winds spread all the way down the strait if the pressure-slope turns more toward the north. These winds are a "pushed" wind that can develop at any time of the year when a small ridge of high pressure develops over the Fraser Valley and along the Cascade Mountains. The winds tend to be stronger along the Vancouver Island side of the Strait of Georgia than along the mainland coast.

With a ridge of high pressure to the north of the region, northwest winds blow down the strait and turn through the Gulf and San Juan Islands, and into Juan de Fuca Strait as northeasterlies. Race Rocks will report northeast winds, while Sheringham, a little farther to the west will report lighter easterly winds. The winds hit the Olympic Mountains and run westward along the American shore and are reported by Tatoosh Island, at the mouth of Juan de Fuca Strait. During a strong winter outflow when the winds come out from the Fraser Valley (a northeast pressure-slope) the winds at Tatoosh Island will frequently rise to gale force overnight and in the early morning hours. The western end of this plume of winds is drawn over to the Canadian side of the strait during the following morning, and is reported as a southeast wind of 20 to 25 knots at Carmanah Point. This oscillation of the easterly plume has been given the name "Carmanah wobble." Sometimes the plume will bend back far enough to the east that the winds at Sheringham rise to 15 to 20 knots. This pattern will be repeated for several days if the outflow pattern continues. At other times, however, it will be a one day event just before the approach of a front.

The northwest winds that develop in the Strait of Georgia with a northerly pressure-slope tend to last for several days. During the summer the winds ease in the north in the afternoon but if there is enough heating in the Fraser

Valley, sea breeze effects will maintain strong northwest winds of 20 to 25 knots off Vancouver. When the air is colder and the outflow is strong, the winds may persist throughout the day with little afternoon easing. Overall the amount of easing is less than with northwest winds created by a westerly pressure-slope.

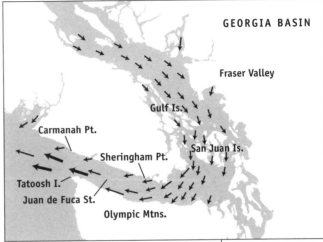

GEORGIA BASIN

Fraser Valley

Gulf Is.

Carmanah Pt.

Sheringham Pt.

San Juan Is.

Tatoosh I.

Juan de Fuca St.

Olympic Mtns.

Winds through the inlets are from the north, and increase in strength as the pressure-slope gradient increases. The strongest winds occur when a strong ridge lies over the BC interior and cold arctic air spills out onto the coast. Winds during a strong arctic outflow rise to gale to storm force, and infrequently to hurricane force. These strong winds are normally confined to the inlets but occasionally spill out a short distance beyond their mouths. As the pressure-slope turns toward the northeast, strong northeast winds begin to pour out of the Fraser Valley and move across the Gulf and San Juan Islands and into the eastern parts of Juan de Fuca Strait. Gale force northeast winds are common at Race Rocks in this situation.

A hurricane force wind of 64 knots was recorded at Pam Rocks in Howe Sound on 20 March 2002. That was the highest wind recorded at that site. Likely, stronger and more frequent hurricane force winds occur in Bute Inlet, but there is no site that records them.

The northerly winds in the inlets may ease to light during a summer afternoon, but the amount of diurnal easing is less in spring and autumn, and almost non-existent in winter. A strong arctic outflow can create freezing spray even in Howe Sound, the most southerly of the coastal inlets. In the mid-1980s, when there was a buoy at Pam Rocks to measure the winds, the buoy almost sank due to the weight of accumulated icing.

SOUTHERLY PRESSURE-SLOPE WINDS

A wide variety of changes take place in the winds across the Georgia basin when the pressure-slope ranges between 130° and 200°. These usually coincide

with the approach and passage of a front across the region. The first change occurs near 130°, as southwest winds start pouring into Juan de Fuca Strait. As the pressure-slope turns more toward the south the winds move up across the Gulf and San Juan Islands, and cause a shift of winds in Howe Sound, from moderate northerly to moderate to strong southerly. Only the southern parts of the Strait of Georgia see southerly winds. The winds over the northern strait don't turn into the south but shift from south-

east to northwest. With very strong pressure rises behind a front the southwest winds may approach gale force very briefly over the southern parts of the Strait of Georgia.

A similar pattern also develops in the same range of pressure-slopes, but this time when the rotation is not from east to south, but from west to south. This happens when a ridge of high pressure lies west of the region and is being pushed inland ahead of an approaching front. Westerly winds are strong in Juan de Fuca Strait in the afternoon, and northwest winds are blowing in the Strait of Georgia. As the ridge moves over Juan de Fuca Strait the pressure-slope backs toward the south, and in some cases as far as southeast. The westerly winds in Juan de Fuca start to move northward, passing across the San Juan Islands and into southern Strait of Georgia. The winds at Bellingham rise to southerly 10 to 15 knots. East Point is the next to report the southerly winds, and Sand Heads and Merry Island follow soon after. This plume of south to southeast winds usually reaches Merry Island overnight, or in the early morning, then spreads over to the Vancouver Island side of the strait later in the morning. The winds rise to 20 knots as they pass Ballenas and Sisters islands. The forecasters at the Pacific Weather Centre call this a "Juan de Fuca return flow."

A local southerly wind, which occurs in this range of pressure-slopes, has become so famous that its name is often applied to any southerly wind in the Georgia Basin. This is the "Qualicum" wind that begins in Port Alberni Inlet, and passes over the top of Vancouver Island to come down onto the water just off Qualicum Beach. The wind may start as a sea breeze in the Port Alberni Inlet, but is propelled across the island by the pressure difference between the west and east sides. Like the Juan de Fuca return flow, it also occurs just ahead of a small ridge, which forms ahead of an approaching front. The Qualicum wind can extend to Lasqueti Island, funnelling up through False Bay and blasting down into Scottie Bay. Normally, only the

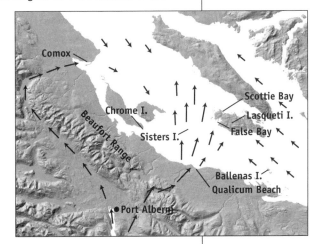

Qualicum wind, or the Juan de Fuca return flow wind develops at any one time, not both. Light southwest winds have also been reported in Comox Harbour at the same time as a Qualicum wind. It appears that part of the flow from Alberni Inlet passes along the Beaufort Range, over Comox Lake, then into the harbour.

The Qualicum wind typically rises in the evening to southwest 25 knots at Sisters Island. The wind eases overnight but sometimes lasts until the early morning. Qualicum winds generally develop when there are light winds in the Strait of Georgia, but if there is a moderate southeasterly in the strait, the plume of winds that passes over Qualicum Beach will turn north to hit Chrome Island. In the more unusual event when there are northwest winds in the strait, the plume has been known to bend south, and is recorded at Ballenas Island. Similar southwest winds have been observed through other gaps over the southern part of the island.

The inlets have a diurnal southerly inflow in summer. The winds are northerly overnight, which ease in the early morning, then change to a southerly inflow by late morning and strengthen through the afternoon, reaching a peak by late afternoon or early evening. The winds are strongest near the head of the inlet, as many a windsurfer will attest. The winds drop near sunset, and a light northerly outflow again develops overnight.

SOUTH COAST | **GEORGIA BASIN**

WESTERLY PRESSURE-SLOPE WINDS

Westerly winds in the Georgia Basin develop in two basic patterns, either after the passage of a front or with a ridge that has built to the west of the region.

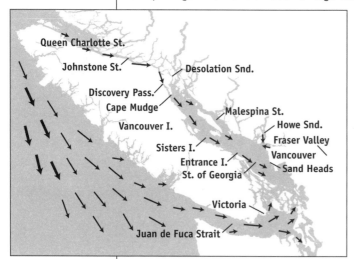

If the pressure rise behind the front is strong, then the northwest winds in the Strait of Georgia and the westerlies in Juan de Fuca Strait will be stronger, often reaching gale force. One of the major problems with these winds is that the wind shift from east to west can be extremely rapid, with speeds going from next to nothing to gale or even storm force in minutes. A shift like this may happen several times during the course of the year. If the front approaches from the northwest the winds that develop behind the front will be equally spread over both sides of the Strait of Georgia but will tend to lean toward the American side in Juan de Fuca Strait. If the front approaches from the southwest, the winds will be stronger on the mainland side of the Strait of Georgia, and along the Canadian side of Juan de Fuca Strait.

While the post-frontal westerlies are predominantly an autumn and winter phenomenon, the ridge westerlies are common in spring and summer. The summer westerly winds have a strong diurnal cycle that begins as a sea breeze in Queen Charlotte Strait during the afternoon, and proceeds through Johnstone Strait in the early evening. The winds then pass through Discovery Passage and out past Cape Mudge in the late evening, before midnight, and work their way down the Strait of Georgia to the Sand Heads area in the early morning hours, before daybreak. These winds pass down the Vancouver Island side of the strait overnight, and don't spread over to the Sunshine Coast until morning. The winds funnel through Malaspina Strait during the afternoon but do not usually create serious conditions. When there is a small ridge over the Fraser Valley with pressure values at least as high as over the central part of the Strait of Georgia, then the northwest winds may stop near Entrance Island.

The westerly winds in Juan de Fuca Strait can have aspects of either being pushed by higher pressures to the west, or drawn by falling pressure caused by summertime afternoon heating over the mainland coast. Typically, summer westerly winds rise to 25 to 30 knots by late afternoon or early evening, and gale force 35 knots are not uncommon. These winds die down overnight, or at latest in the early morning, and start to rise again in the late morning.

The mainland inlets do not get westerly winds with any strength due to their alignment. Westerly winds move into the western parts of Desolation Sound but do not reach the eastern areas. The eastern areas may, however, get westerly winds where afternoon sea breeze winds are from the west.

Topography is very important in the formation of local winds. Take note of the topography in your area and observe how the local winds relate to it.

Chatham Point to Port Hardy

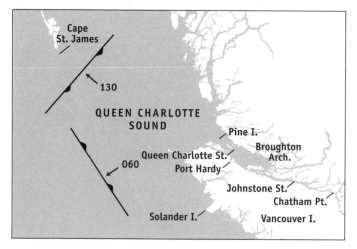

Mariners often keep a good watch on their barometer for rapid pressure drops. The pressure may also drop with the arrival of the surge of stratus and fog moving up from the Washington coast.

EASTERLY PRESSURE-SLOPE WINDS

Queen Charlotte Strait

When a front approaches this region the winds shift to an easterly direction with the pressure-slope lying between 060° and 130°. The exact angle of the pressure-slope will determine where the winds will be strongest, and where they may not blow at all. When the front approaches from the northwest the pressure-slope will be closer to 130°, and the winds will be strongest through the central and northern parts of Queen Charlotte Strait, and will enter the southern sections of the Broughton Archipelago. When the front approaches from the southwest, the pressure-slope is closer to 060° and the winds will be strongest on the Vancouver Island side of the strait. The winds will remain light through most of Johnstone Strait when the pressure-slope is near 060°, but rise when the pressure-slope turns toward 130°, which happens as the front draws near.

When a front approaches from the northwest the winds in Queen Charlotte Strait will shift from southeast to west about 6 or 7 hours after it shifts at Cape St. James. When a front approaches from the southwest the wind shift that occurs at Cape St. James, or Solander Island will take place near Port Hardy only an hour later. However, sometimes a front will stall over Queen Charlotte Sound, and may take days before it crosses Queen Charlotte Strait, if ever.

The sea conditions through the strait arise primarily from wind-generated waves, and from their interaction with tidal currents. Tides play a very signifi-

cant part in the sea state, for when the tidal currents run against the winds the seas become shorter and sharper, and can build up to a metre higher than what they would be without the opposition of winds and tides. The wind waves are largely fetch limited. If the winds were a steady 40 knots throughout the 45 nautical miles from the eastern end of Queen Charlotte Strait to Pine Island the seas would vary from less than one metre in the east to about 3.5 metres at Pine Island.

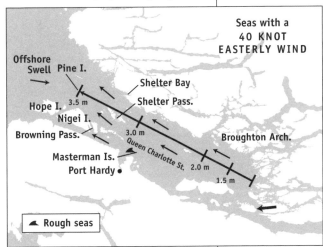

Western Queen Charlotte Strait during a storm offers no shelter between Shelter Bay on the north shore, and Hope and Nigei islands on the south. These islands may provide shelter in some situations, depending on the direction of the wind. The passageways between the islands, such as Shelter Passage and Browning Passage, may have even stronger winds due to funnelling when the winds become southerly.

Sea conditions near the Masterman Islands, off Port Hardy, are notoriously nasty with strong easterly winds. Tides between Masterman Islands and Pulteney Point are strong. Swells from distant storms bend around the top of Vancouver Island and enter Queen Charlotte Strait, but their impact is confined to the northern shore and the southern Broughton Archipelago.

Broughton Archipelago

Strong southeast winds in Queen Charlotte Strait hit along the edge of the Broughton Archipelago when the pressure-slope is east or southeast, but do not spread with the same strength through the waters within the archipelago. This means that winds may be strong at the mouth of Arrow Passage, Fife Sound, and Wells Passage but are not terribly strong farther up in the waterways. Drury Inlet, Sutlej Channel, and Penphrase Passage, which are oriented toward the southeast, get stronger winds, but since the fetch is limited the seas are choppy but not rough.

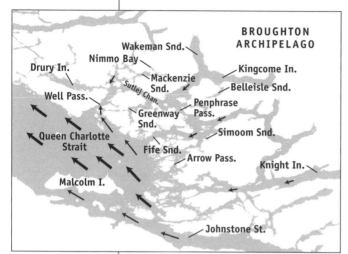

Locally gusty winds will occur in various inlets such as Simoom Sound, Belleisle Sound, Nimmo Bay off Mackenzie Sound, and Greenway Sound, as southeast winds aloft come down off the mountains. Areas that are less mountainous do not have problems with downslope gusty winds. Sailors call the steadier, less gusty winds "clean" winds, for they are smoother, and sails pull better.

When the pressure-slope is from the northeast there will be light outflow winds through some passages, though the winds in Queen Charlotte Strait may be strong southeast. When it turns more northerly and becomes colder, as it does from December through March, most waters within the Broughton Archipelago will be glassy calm. Only those waters that have connections to northerly outflow will experience much wind.

Johnstone Strait

After the passage of a front the winds in Johnstone Strait ease and try to shift into the southwest, but because of the confined channels of the strait

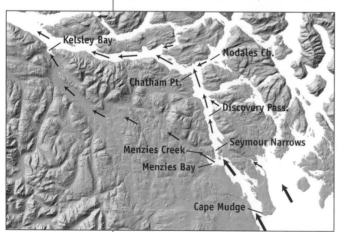

they don't change direction but ease to light. The winds aloft, however, will shift into the southwest, and these upper winds may in some locations interact with the mountaintops to produce downdrafts, giving strong and gusty surface winds.

In Discovery Passage the southeast winds are strongest on the western side of the passage, up to Menzies Bay and Seymour Narrows. With a flooding tide the west side of this passage should be avoided. The winds tend to ease just north of Seymour Narrows, as some of the winds crossing Menzies Bay pass up

Menzies Creek. The winds may strengthen again near Chatham Point, due to corner effects around the point, plus the addition of winds coming out Nodales Channel.

> Strong southeast winds against a rising (flooding) tide in Johnstone Strait will produce seas that are over a metre higher than with an ebb or slack tide. Waves in Johnstone Strait quickly subside after the winds drop, and when the tide runs against them.

NORTHERLY PRESSURE-SLOPE WINDS

Knight Inlet, like the other coastal inlets that experience outflow winds, has its own peculiarities. The arctic air spreads from the Chilcotin area of the BC interior down the Klinaklini River valley, and forms a wall of northerlies as it enters the head of Knight Inlet. It creates "a wild piece of wind" at corners such as Cascade Point. The winds that pass through Bute Inlet also originate in the Chilcotin Plateau, but exit via the Hamathko River valley. Both rivers pass through mountain glacier fields that add cold drainage winds to the strength of the outflow.

The northeast outflow winds, as they pour through Knight Inlet, flow like a river, bouncing off one side then the other. Some relief from moderate northerly winds may be found in the bays just south of Transit Head, south of Kwalate Point, and in Hoeya Sound. In the strongest outflow events, however, the winds fan out into most bays so that there is no place to hide. In these events the winds are non-stop, creating a steady roar, from the head of the inlet

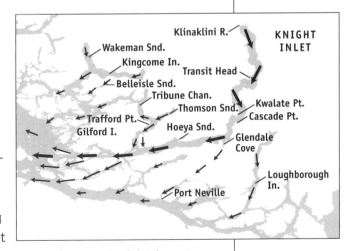

to Glendale Cove. It has been said that you cannot go up the inlet in a strong outflow. There are very few places to anchor. The outflow has been noted to ease, in some cases, from Hoeya Sound toward the mouth of the inlet.

SOUTH COAST | **CHATHAM POINT TO PORT HARDY**

> There are no reporting sites to indicate the strength of winds in Knight Inlet, but it has been suggested that the wind strength is similar to that at Cathedral Point in Burke Channel - which is included on the continuous marine broadcasts.

The outflow winds from Knight Inlet fan out into the various channels at its mouth with somewhat reduced speeds. The main thrust of the outflow passes south of Midsummer Island and out toward Malcolm Island, and hits hard on Donegal Head. Large seas are created with outflow winds south of Malcolm Island, but the winds are hardly noticeable north of the island. They funnel into Cormorant Channel, just north of Cormorant Island, and can be especially bad near the Haddington Reefs. The winds south of Ledge Point may be 5 or 10 knots stronger than near Rough Bay on Malcolm Island.

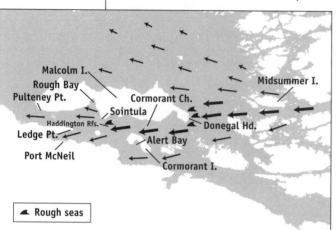

Easterly winds pass south of Cormorant Island, but Alert Bay will have lee protection. In the strongest outflow events the winds extend all the way west along Vancouver Island to Port Hardy, and are recorded at Scarlet Point.

After several days of outflow, during which time the depth of the cold air increases, the outflow begins to take other paths out to the coast. The cold air moves into Loughborough Inlet and out into Johnstone Strait. It will also pass from Knight Inlet, over Glendale Cove, and into Port Neville. Northeast winds also make it over the mountains and into Thompson Sound. Winds of 60 knots have been experienced at the mouth of the sound, near Trafford Point. The strength of these winds is reportedly strongest in January, but is generally much less than in Knight Inlet.

> Some mariners try to get a forewarning of northeast outflow winds by listening to reports of weather in Alberta or northeastern BC. If the temperature drops, then they know an outflow is coming.

Lesser northerly outflow winds travel down along the backside of Gilford Island. Some of these winds also spread west from Trafford Point into Tribune Channel.

Kingcome Inlet also experiences outflow winds that must be partially drainage winds from the Mt. Waddington Glacier, but since it does not have an open passageway into the BC interior, the winds are not extreme. Some of the Kingcome outflow winds pass through Belleisle Sound. Wakeman Sound likely receives some outflow winds, which merge with the outflow in Kingcome Inlet. Wells Passage and Drury Inlet have some

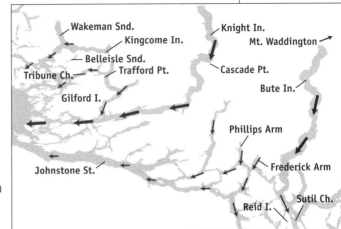

outflow winds, but they are a mere hint of the strength that occurs through Knight Inlet.

Bute outflow winds, as mentioned in *The Wind Came All Ways*, are fierce, and warrant full respect. The main thrust of the Bute winds passes the top end of Reid Island, and out into Sutil Channel. During the most severe arctic outbreaks, when the depth of cold air increases sufficiently to move over higher passes, winds will start to pass through several nearby passageways such as Frederick Arm and Phillips Arm, and then out through various channels into Johnstone Strait. But by the time it reaches these associated channels, the full ferocity of the outflow winds is significantly reduced. Both Bute and Knight inlets can ice up, though not so solid that it requires an icebreaker to pass through, but a surface coating is created that reduces wave development.

> The strong outflow winds create dangerous conditions near the mouth of the inlets when they run against an incoming tide.

During the initial outbreak of the cold arctic winds, there may still be sufficient clouds around for snow to fall. Later, once the ridge has built over the area and the cold air is fully established, it becomes sunny. Additional snowfall may occur when a weather system moves off the Pacific, bringing enough moisture for clouds to form. The transition from arctic cold to the normal mild Pacific weather can see local periods of freezing rain at the heads of inlets where the cold air is trapped. One mariner summed this up by saying, "all kinds of weather are possible during the winter in the Broughton Archipelago. The weather can be beautiful with a flat, glassy calm, but there can also be strong winds, turbulence, rain, and snow. The snow line can drop down to the water."

Wakeman Sound and the upper parts of Kingcome Inlet can both freeze over in winter. The waterfalls can freeze up along Knight Inlet, all the way down to Cascade Point (locally called Twin Falls). The more significant icing problem, though, is not surface water ice, but freezing spray. Some mariners said that the outflow is not as strong, nor as widespread, as it has been in the past, for ice from freezing spray used to form on boats in Queen Charlotte Strait.

SOUTHERLY PRESSURE-SLOPE WINDS

Southwest winds are generally only experienced in the western, more open, parts of Queen Charlotte Strait, and in some channels in the Broughton Archipelago that are open to the south. The only place in the Johnstone Strait area where they occur is through Discovery Passage, and locally out smaller inlets such as near Kelsey Bay. With strong southwest winds aloft at mountain-top heights that are capped with an inversion above, the flow may sometimes interact with the mountain and surge downwards onto the water. These winds occur in a number of places throughout the Broughton Archipelago.

SOUTHWEST WINDS AGAINST A TIDAL OUTFLOW

Belize In.
Slingsby Chan.
Nakwakto Rpds.
Nugent Snd.
Tidal Outflow
Seymour In.
Storm I.

Seymour Channel, Nugent Sound, and Belize Inlet all empty their tidal waters through narrow Slingsby Channel. As a result, the outgoing flow is very strong. When this outgoing tide is against a west or southwest wind the conditions can be very rough. The plume fans out after leaving the inlet but while the strength eases it creates an even larger area of rough waters, which may extend all the way out to the Storm Islands.

Nakwakto Rapids, lying between Seymour Inlet and Slingsby Channel, reaches speeds of 16 knots on an ebb, which is one of the strongest tidal streams in the world. You can only safely navigate these rapids at slack water, which lasts just six minutes.

South or southwest winds in Queen Charlotte Strait are often called Nimpkish winds, even if not all southerly winds pass through the Nimpkish Valley. This is similar to the Strait of Georgia where southerly winds are called Qualicum winds, even if they do not originate in the Qualicum Valley. The classic Nimpkish winds are those caused by daytime heating within the Nimpkish Valley, from spring to early autumn. As the air is heated along the valley sides it rises upward, and is replaced by winds travelling from the south along the lake. The surface winds will reach 30 knots at times. Some of the

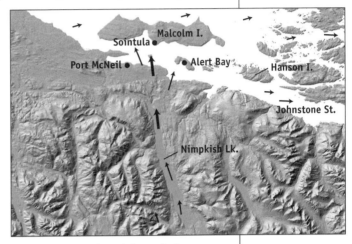

wind spills out of the valley to hit Alert Bay and Sointula, giving wind speeds of 10 to 20 knots. When there is a ridge west of Vancouver Island, and lower pressure in Queen Charlotte Strait, the winds also get a push from the pressure difference.

The Nimpkish Valley extends south from Port McNeil. In it lies the 22km long Nimpkish Lake, which is one of the better windsurfing sites in North America.

The strongest south to southwest winds, however, are not due to daytime heating, but rather to strong pressure rises behind a front. The Nimpkish Valley funnels these winds to much greater speeds. These stronger winds seem to be most common from April to June, but can occur at other times of the year. Southerly winds of 50 knots have occurred in this area, downwind of the Nimpkish Valley, and extreme winds of 85 knots have been reported. While these winds are usually only a puff, they can in the most extreme cases last for several hours. Several mariners said that they have not experienced a Nimpkish wind of legendary strength for fifteen years or more.

In inlets that are not aligned to the southwest, the southerly winds behind the front are not usually a concern, for they tend to go up over the inlet. Local turbulence, and even whirlwinds (waterspouts), have been reported off the steep south side of Hanson Island, where the winds are deflected and spun. Similar conditions likely occur elsewhere in the region. Depending on the topography the winds may be confined to narrow plumes, which show at a distance as a black streak on the water, with glassy calm water on either side.

WESTERLY PRESSURE-SLOPE WINDS

Post-frontal westerlies

Most summer westerly winds are primarily associated with a weak ridge of high pressure offshore, and sea breeze effects. Stronger westerly winds can also occur during the summer months, either associated with a strong ridge of high pressure offshore, or following the passage of a front. Winds can rise rapidly behind a front if the pressure rises rapidly, but the strong winds are usually brief, for the pressure difference equalizes quickly.

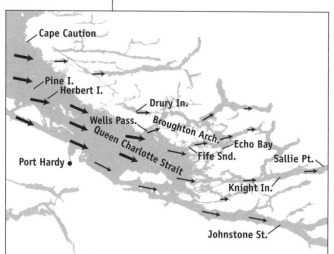

During our crossing past Cape Caution on 4 May 2001, the Kabirian experienced strong post-frontal winds. The winds at Herbert Island shifted in minutes from southeast 26 knots to westerly 28 knots with gusts to 35. The pressure rose almost six millibars in the three hours after the passage of the front. The winds funnelled through the islands of the Broughton Archipelago, and rose to southwest 45 knots in Echo Bay. Southwest winds can be dangerous, for they can be fast and furious.

Westerly winds that develop after the passage of a front are not linked with diurnal heating, for the fronts can pass at any time of the day, so they do not regularly go down with the sun. Many storms follow the pattern of a low moving north into the Gulf of Alaska with a front crossing the region. But before the southeast winds ahead of the front shift all the way into the north-west, a secondary trough, which extends southwest from the low, has to pass. The interval between the passage of the first front, and the arrival of the trough, is often about one full day. This provides a period of relative calm. Clouds may lift but do not always clear, until the trough has passed.

> One mariner commented that if a clear band appears on the horizon just before sunset, then nine times out of ten, the winds shift, and rise to northwest 40 knots by midnight. This timing has not been noticed by forecasters in the weather office, but is possible and should be watched for and recorded.

Westerly winds spread fairly evenly throughout the region, and are much the same strength on both sides of the strait. They will spread into all the inlets that open toward the west or southwest, such as Wells Passage, Drury Inlet, and Fife Sound. The strength of the winds in these inlets will be increased through funnelling, or reduced by blocking terrain. If strong westerlies arrive at the mouth of inlets, such as Knight Inlet, while diurnal outflow winds are occurring, then steeper, more dangerous seas result. Westerlies that are caused by a strong ridge of high pressure offshore, and not just by sea breeze effects, usually move up Knight Inlet as far as Sallie Point.

Diurnal cycle of winds

A ridge of high pressure west of Vancouver Island gives a general westerly flow pattern. The strength of the winds varies depending on the exact position and strength of the ridge. They do not blow continuously, but have a daily breathing rhythm caused by daytime heating over the adjacent land. They act much like a sea breeze, for they increase with the heating of the day, and end as the sun goes down. In the peak of the summer much of the wind variations are caused by local differences in the amount of heating that one place receives compared to a neighbouring place. Local heating effects can be more important than passing weather systems during the summer.

Westerly winds will begin around 1000 hours if there is no fog overnight, but are delayed until 1200 or 1300 if the fog is slow to burn off. The winds normally rise to about 15 knots in Queen Charlotte Strait during the afternoon with local winds to 20. They reach their peak around 1500 to 1600 hours, then

Mariners have noted that strong winds can occasionally be seen at the top of their mast during the morning while the winds on the water remain quiet.

quickly ease to light near sunset. It is generally said that the warmer the day, the stronger the winds. A cloudy day may not see strong winds at all. Overnight, once the fog reforms, the light westerly winds may shift to light easterlies.

> Blackfish Sound, just east of Malcolm Island had nine days in a row in August 1974 with westerly winds over 35 knots. While westerly winds are common in August, these winds were stronger than normal, and didn't let up.

Summer westerlies at the western end of Queen Charlotte Strait are never very strong. They are not much more than a light sea breeze giving winds of 10 to 15 knots. The westerlies moving into Wells Passage can reach 20 knots near the junction with Sutlej Channel. Inflow, sea breeze type winds occur through the rest of the channels on the northern side of Queen Charlotte Strait but are very local in nature, and generally not strong. Westerly winds funnel around Broughton Island creating gusty, turbulent airs on the north side, in Greenway Sound.

The summer westerlies are a little stronger on the north side of Malcolm Island than to the south. Sailors report that the winds are "cleanest" near Pulteney Point, having few gusts and eddies, hence allowing the sail to pull more strongly. Westerlies cross over the isthmus near Port McNeil so the best place to anchor is just south of Ledge Point. The westerly winds "bunch up" over the eastern areas, northeast of Malcolm Island, and toward the opening of Johnstone Strait. The winds are noticeably stronger at White Cliff Islets. They also funnel into Arrow Passage then Cramer Passage, but there is some shelter in the Fox group of islands and little westerly wind moves into Retreat Passage.

The winds start picking up in western Johnstone Strait, off West Cracroft Island, and are worst near Kelsey Bay. The westerly winds are strengthened as they funnel eastward into the narrower passageway of Johnstone Strait. The onset and ending times are later the farther east you go. At Chatham Point, for

128

instance, they usually don't start until around 1500 hours, and reach their peak in the evening, sometimes close to midnight. Whenever the sun is shining you can expect the westerly winds to form and rise to 25 to 30 knots at Chatham Point with a westerly pressure-slope. Winds of gale force 35 to 40 knots are not uncommon. Occasionally the winds last through the night, and die down in the early morning.

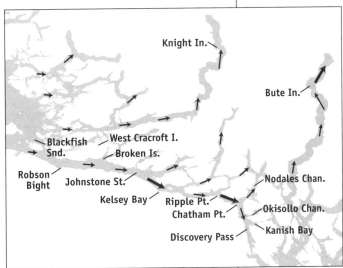

After the flow of westerly winds passes Kelsey Bay it eases, but then increases again, reaching a peak near Ripple Point, a little west of Chatham Point. Often it appears that the winds at Ripple Point are about 10 knots stronger that just off Chatham Point. Winds of 15 to 20 knots at Herbert Island in the western Queen Charlotte Strait result in 25 to 30 knot winds near Chatham Point, with occasional winds reaching gales 35 to 40 knots. These winds ease after passing Chatham Point, once the strait splits into several channels. Little of the westerly winds moves into Nodales Channel, except after a three-day blow, when the westerly winds go everywhere, but even then they generally don't go beyond Brougham Point. Most of the westerlies turn down into Discovery Passage. Kanish Bay gets some of this flow, but little goes into Okisollo Channel.

Fog

In the late summer and early autumn a large bank of fog forms to the north of Vancouver Island, close to the central coast, and extends south into Queen Charlotte Strait. The initial approach of the fog can be very sudden so mariners should keep a sharp look out for it. The fog spreads through the strait and into most inlets, but generally does not extend much farther east than Robson Bight, in Johnstone Strait. It is an advection fog that forms when warm moist air blows over colder water. The fog does not extend inland, as the air over land is hotter and drier than over the water.

The fog goes through a daily cycle of burning off during the day and reforming overnight. The clearing begins near the coast, where the air warms up fastest, and spreads toward the centre of the strait. On the first day of fog, it usually burns off before 1000, but every day it takes longer as the fog gets thicker, so after a few days it may be 1200 or 1300 before it finally clears. Fog patches may persist in the centre of the strait through the day. The fog penetrates farther into Johnstone Strait and up the inlets with each passing day. The inlets start clearing at their heads around 1000, and clearing reaches their openings an hour or two later. It usually takes three days before the fog creates a major problem.

If cloud covers the fog, daytime heating will not be as strong, and the fog may not burn off and can persist for days. Blackfish Sound once had fog for 16 days in a row. Winds are generally light in the fog, but increase as the fog lifts. The fog reforms soon after the winds ease during the evening. If the winds continue until midnight, then the fog doesn't reform until near 0400. If the winds continue through the night, but die in the early morning, the fog forms instantly around 0700 or 0800. Mariners have noted that when fog doesn't dissipate but lifts into stratocumulus clouds in the morning, you may get rain by afternoon.

Local coastal phenomena may also cause some areas to have more persistent fog, while other areas tend to avoid it altogether. An example of this is seen when the fog spreads toward the bank at the end of Malcolm Island, for the fog normally turns out again, leaving a hole in the fog bank, just off Sointula. These clear areas may be caused by local pockets of warmer water, or by winds that blow off the drier land.

Inlet winds

During the summer the winds generally blow up the coastal inlets during the late morning and afternoon. The strength of these inflow winds is greater in the inlets that have more gentle slopes, for they heat up more strongly. The inflow winds switch into a light outflow during the night. In the early days of summer, before much of the snow melts off the mountains, the outflow winds are strong since there is a sharp temperature contrast between the snow-capped mountains and the lower parts of the inlets. The winds can rise abruptly in the evening. The seas increase over the shallow bars near the mouth of the inlets. They should only be crossed when running with the tide. Summer outflow winds die away in the morning as the temperature rises.

> Near the head of Knight Inlet cold winds coming down off the glaciers persist as the afternoon southerly inflow winds strengthen. Waterspouts sometimes form where these two winds meet - they are not "killers," but impressive none the less.

Kelsey Bay winds

Kelsey Bay winds are the "Brooks Peninsula winds" of the inside passage. In summer the westerly winds that run through Johnstone Strait are strengthened as they pass Hickey Point, reaching their peak off Kelsey Bay, before easing again just west of Race Passage. The explanation for these winds is somewhat uncertain but they appear to be caused by interaction with Newcastle Ridge. There is a slight bend in Johnstone Strait near Hickey Point so the westerly winds increase through corner effects as they pass Newcastle Ridge. There might also be additional downslope effects with upper level winds coming down off Newcastle Ridge, just east of Hickey Point. The winds are cold after passing over the snow-covered mountain so bend in a wavelike fashion and flow downward towards the sea.

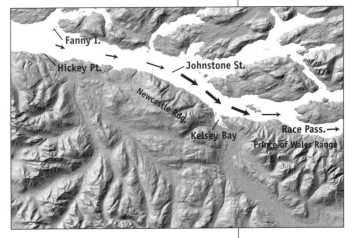

At Hickey Point, the winds may be only 15 to 20 knots while they could be gale force, or higher, at Kelsey Bay. Fanny Island, the nearest wind-recording site to Kelsey Bay, would likely report 20 to 25 knots, when Kelsey Bay has gale force winds. Normally the peak winds off Kelsey Bay are less than 40 knots, but old-timers have seen westerly squalls up to 100 knots. When winds of anywhere near this magnitude are against the tides, horrendous seas develop, forming a veritable wall of water. Twenty-foot seas have been observed off the government dock at Kelsey Bay. One mariner noted that strong Kelsey Bay winds occur when it is clear, and there is a "cap" cloud over the Prince of Wales Range. It is not a problem if the clouds are just drifting over the mountain, but when the clouds remain stationary over the mountain then look out - strong winds are almost guaranteed. The most favoured time for these winds is May to early July, when there is a significant amount of snow on its peak.

> It is possible to avoid travelling past Kelsey Bay by taking a route through the many passages north of Johnstone Strait, from Sutil Channel to Sunderland Channel.

In a 1965 storm force winds moved up the Zeballos Inlet hitting the east side so hard that you couldn't stand up in the wind. It had been raining for days and water started going up the cliff side.

North Vancouver Island

EASTERLY PRESSURE-SLOPE WINDS

Port Hardy to Winter Harbour

Leaving Port Hardy for the west side of Vancouver Island requires a bit of planning for there are few places to hide from strong southeast winds until you get into Quatsino Sound. In addition to the potential for strong winds off the end of the island, Nahwitti Bar and near Cape Scott are notorious for producing very nasty seas. Nahwitti Bar is bad when the tide is against the winds. It is quite shallow over the bar so the seas build amazingly, but once past the bar it is generally okay. The tides are again bad when against the 1½-3 knot currents off Cape Scott, and produce dangerous rips and overfalls.

> Nahwitti Bar like Cape Caution to the north, requires full respect. Crossing the bar requires timing, for both the weather and the tides need to be just right. When they are, it is a breeze, and you will wonder what the big fuss is about Nahwitti Bar, but if they are not both right then you will quickly wish you were somewhere else.

To avoid crossing the shallows of Nahwitti Bar, take the route through Gordan Channel and out well past Hope Island before turning west. To avoid the over-falls near Cape Scott you need to go farther out, close to Cox Island before turning south. Generally the tidal currents on the west side of Vancouver Island are less than those inside. They only peak near 1½ knots, but are strong in some local areas such as near the outer Scott Islands where the tides are described as "running like a river."

Goletas Channel and Nahwitti Bar are sometimes very quiet, but at other times blow hard southeast. In the storm of 26 October 2001 when hurricane force winds were reported at Solander and Sartine islands, and also in Queen Charlotte Sound, the winds were reported to be above 80 knots in Goletas Channel. Bate Passage may provide some relief with certain wind directions but in others it will be as strong or stronger than in Goletas Channel.

Southeast winds, as seen in the radar wind images in Chapter 3, blow on both sides of northern Vancouver Island, and create an area of lighter winds off Cape Scott, with a line of stronger winds extending farther out where the two streams converge. With very slight variations in direction of the southeast winds, this line is seen to move from one side of Cape Scott to the other. While the winds can be very strong they are generally less than the winds at Solander, which are strengthened by corner effects around the Brooks Peninsula.

Coastal effects can dramatically change the conditions over very short distances. Inside bays such as San Josef Bay, southeast winds are usually a lot lighter than just outside the bay. Sea Otter Cove, however, which is just next to San Josef Bay, can get strong winds.

Quatsino Sound

With the approach of most lows and fronts, the winds in Quatsino Sound begin as light northeasters. The Quatsino light station on Kains Island will remain light northeast long after winds even just a mile offshore have risen to strong or gale force southeasterlies. The full strength of the winds is said to go overtop of the community of Quatsino. Winds inside the sound will generally not rise above 30 knots, during times when 50 knots are being reported in Queen Charlotte Strait, and 60 knots at Solander Island. Because of this sheltering, Quatsino Sound has been referred to as a "pond" that is in most situations separated from the wild winds offshore.

When the pressure-slope is close to southeast, the southeast winds accelerate around Lawn Point and move into the opening of Quatsino Sound, but these strong winds do not spread throughout the sound with the same strength. The southeast winds that do spread into the sound generally do so when the air is stable. At this time, the winds will be steady and not gusty. If the southeast winds occur during an outgoing tide (which can be as high as four metres) then huge seas will develop at the mouth of Quatsino Inlet. The seas are particularly nasty in the stretch from Kwakiutl Point to Kains Island.

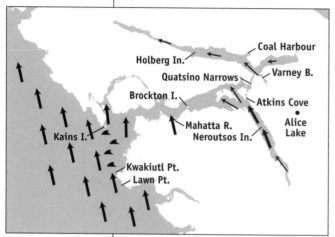

The strongest of the southeast winds occurs near the mouth of the sound, off Mahatta River, and in Neroutsos Inlet. Off Mahatta River the wind spills out in a narrow plume, not much more than a mile wide. The winds are light on either side of the plume. In Neroutsos Inlet the southeast winds are generally stronger, hitting particularly hard near Atkins Cove. Some wind turns up through Quatsino Narrows and into Holberg Inlet, but it is less strong than in Neroutsos Inlet. Holberg tends to receive most of its southeast wind from Varney Bay, which is open to the shallow land near Alice Lake. The gentle slopes of Holberg Inlet do not cause the winds to funnel as they do in the steep-sided Neroutsos Inlet. They do get some gusty winds, though, if the angle is just right.

Wind gusts as high as 100 knots have been reported at the end of Neroutsos Inlet, and on one occasion the winds were so strong that a tug lost his windows while bucking into the wind. These winds only occur with what one mariner called "a true southeast." It appears that the "true" southeast is one in which the pressure-slope is not east or northeast, but closer to southeast. When this extreme wind occurs, the flow is drawn all the way from Kyuquot Sound and through various valleys, before moving into Neroutsos Inlet. The winds shift regularly into the south after the passage of a front, but the strength of the flow at that time is generally reduced so it doesn't cause these notable winds. What is likely needed for this wind to develop is the passage of a low near Cape Scott, with strong pressure rises behind it, and a strong southerly gradient on its southern flank.

Swells from the ocean can move into the sound, especially when the seas are very big offshore and come from a westerly direction. They weaken as they proceed inward, and generally end a little past Brockton Island so little swell passes through Quatsino Narrows into Holberg Inlet.

AVIATORS COMMENTS - Mechanical turbulence can be a problem during periods when north-east outflow winds shift to southeast. This is generally worst near the change of seasons in late November or December, and in March/April. The seasons shift according to changes in water temperatures. When the water temperatures remain warm longer than normal the season changes can be delayed by almost a month.

Brooks Peninsula

Brooks Peninsula has earned the respect of all mariners and aviators who pass near it. It is said that it creates its own weather. It is a massive peninsula that sticks out almost 20 miles from the main part of Vancouver Island and rises to 800 metres above the water surface. It causes such an interruption to the pass- ing flow of both air and water that it creates a variety of very significant coastal effects. A

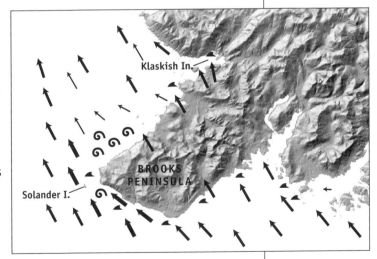

windward, or front-face effect, develops when winds blow directly against the face of the peninsula and back into the east or southeast as they run along the peninsula. This creates turbulent air with marked swirls that develop where the easterly winds mix with the more southerly winds farther offshore. The seas, as a result, are very chaotic.

Corner effects have been known and discussed for many years. This involves winds being strengthened by being forced around an obstacle. Solander Island

135

is the windiest place on the coast because of this effect. Lee-side eddies, which can be severe, are created as the wind passes around the end of the peninsula.

> The geological history of Brooks Peninsula is quite fascinating. Originally, it was not part of the Vancouver Island continental plate, but was part of the oceanic plate that merged with Vancouver Island. It is thought that the peninsula is part of three different plates, including one that moved up from Oregon.

When the air is stable most of the southeast winds that stream up against Brooks Peninsula will be steered around it. The north side of the peninsula is sheltered from some of the streaming air, and as a result, an area of lower pressure is created, a mini-vacuum, so to speak. The air that travels over the peninsula is sucked down by the lower pressure to create strong downward winds.

Klaskish Inlet is notorious for these downward moving winds. One mariner said that "the air plunges into the sea with such an explosive force that the water is thrown some 100 metres into the air before falling back again into the same hole it came from." Ships have experienced being pushed down more than a foot. Skiffs have been overturned, and planes crashed because of these down-ward winds. There are no trees at the head of Klaskish Inlet because of the winds. The difficult thing about these winds is that they don't happen all the time. There must be very subtle factors at play that dictate their development. It does happen often enough, however, that the north side of Brooks Peninsula, and Klaskish Inlet in particular, is a place to treat with extreme caution.

NORTHERLY PRESSURE-SLOPE WINDS

Quatsino Sound

Easterly outflow winds from Knight Inlet, when combined with easterly winds in Queen Charlotte Strait, extend out well past Nahwitti Bar. Part of this flow passes over the low land west of Port McNeil and into Rupert Inlet. From Rupert Inlet, the outflow winds pass into Quatsino Sound then out past the Quatsino

> In years past Holberg Inlet would freeze over enough to allow travel on the ice. Icebreakers have had to open up Holberg. In January 1969 Holberg had 18 days in a row with temperatures below -4°C, and of these there were 10 days below -10°C. The lowest temperature was -17.2°C. The lowest temperature recorded at Quatsino since records began in 1895 was -16.7°C in January 1950. Rarely, there will be enough freezing spray to ice up a boat, and take her down.

Lighthouse. Some of the wind passes into Holberg Inlet and exits through San Josef Bay. The winds off the coast would be light between these two outflow plumes. Neroutsos Inlet remains glassy calm. Winter Harbour does not normally receive strong outflow winds except during a cold arctic outflow event that has been blowing for a number of days. The plume of winds that exits Quatsino Sound turns northward if the pressure-slope is more easterly, and southward if the pressure-slope is more northerly. The winds normally die away within 30 or 40 miles of the mouth. When the pressure-slope turns more to the north, the northerly winds from Fitz Hugh Sound extend southward down past Cape Scott.

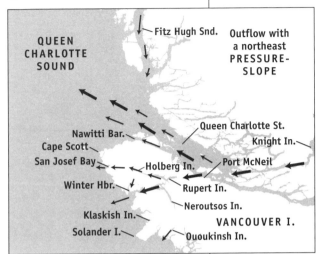

Brooks Peninsula

The winds at Solander Island off Brooks Peninsula are very sensitive to wind directions. Solander will blow from the northwest with full fury but will drop off when the winds turn toward the north. Likewise a northerly wind of 15 to 20 knots can rise to 30 knots in minutes if the wind direction backs by 10 or 20 degrees toward the northwest. The pressure-slope transition point between these two winds is near 300°. During a strong northerly outflow event the winds off Brooks Peninsula remain light, with stronger winds coming out of Quatsino Sound to the north, and out of Kyuquot Sound to the south. Ououkinsh Inlet, just east of Brooks Peninsula, gets some turbulent outflow winds.

SOUTHERLY PRESSURE-SLOPE WINDS

Southwest winds hit hard on the west coast, especially at the heads of inlets that open to the southwest. Sea Otter Cove and San Josef Bay are particularly susceptible. The winds don't last long but can be destructive. The strongest winds occur when a coastal low tracks over northern Vancouver Island. The southerly winds that develop after the low has passed can reach 50 to 60 knots.

In 1897 a group of Danish pioneers established a settlement near Hansen Lagoon and Fisherman Bay. They brought cattle in by boat, and tried to survive by growing crops and fishing. They were promised a road connecting them to Holberg but when that never materialized the continual battle against the elements forced them to give up in 1907. A second attempt was made in 1910 but failed soon after. A few man-made relics and coastal names such as Nels Bight are all that remain.

This sign on the road to Winter Harbour, while intended to warn of logging trucks, could also be used as advice for mariners who ply the waters of the BC coast.

Quatsino Sound

Quatsino Sound is open to the southwest, so it gets both winds and swell from that direction. However, southwest winds don't last long. Fog also spreads up Quatsino Sound with southerly winds.

Because of the shear of winds that occurs from the surface upwards, the winds aloft may be strong southwest but the surface winds would tend to be from the southeast. In this case the winds in Quatsino Sound may be calm at the surface, but strong from the southwest aloft, which is indicated by the fast-moving clouds.

Coal Harbour, near the head of Quatsino Sound, is bad with southwest winds. Carl Botel, an experienced fisherman, and one of the original residents of Winter Harbour, said that "southwest winds come at the tail end of a good southeaster and give one hell of a beating. It is short but strong. Boats slam on the docks. It is almost impossible, then calms down in a half hour. If it happens at a certain point of the tide you will get more than four feet of water over the fingers of the dock - it comes up instantly."

> The Royal Canadian Air Force set up a seaplane base in Coal Harbour in 1940 as part of World War II coastal defences. This site was chosen, at the back door to Port Hardy, because it was thought that if a tsunami were to develop in the Pacific Ocean it would be broken up by Quatsino Narrows before it entered Holberg Inlet. While a tsunami did not occur during the war years, one did occur in 1964 and caused considerable damage at the head of Alberni Inlet, but nothing more than an increased sea level was observed in Coal Harbour.

WESTERLY PRESSURE-SLOPE WINDS

Port Hardy to Winter Harbour

The time to travel around the top end of Vancouver Island in the summer is in the early morning, for northwest winds pick up in the afternoon. Goletas Channel is terrible with westerlies when against an ebbing tide, but once across the Nahwitti Bar it flattens right out. Heavy showers, sometimes with thunder and hail, can develop with westerlies behind a front. Waterspouts have been observed between Topknot Point and Cape Scott in association with these showers.

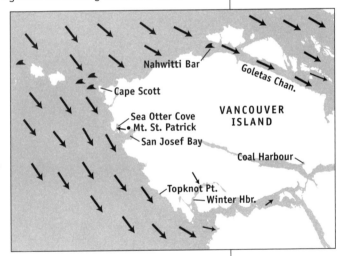

Sea Otter Cove will only get one quarter of the strength of northwest winds that blow offshore. Westerly winds aloft may bounce off Mt. St. Patrick to cause gusty winds to reflect back into Sea Otter Cove, even when there are only light northwest winds offshore. When the pressure-slope is more southwesterly then northwest, winds will go right down the valley from San Josef Bay to give winds to Winter Harbour that are almost as strong as outside.

> When transiting the west side of northern Vancouver Island one mariner said that it is best to stay inside the 100 fathom (200m) line for conditions are usually worse farther outside, but to stay away from canyons near the coast that produce strong upwelling. Also think of how the wind direction may change so that if the winds increase they will be behind you.

Quatsino Sound

When the pressure-slope is westerly, then the winds remain offshore and do not enter Quatsino Sound. When the pressure-slope is southwesterly the northwest winds impact the outer parts of Quatsino Sound and reach down the coast to hit Brooks Peninsula. If the pressure-slope angle is just right, northwest winds can pour into Holberg Inlet to create lumpy seas near Henricksen Point, but generally they are not too troublesome. Some of these winds will occasionally pass over the peninsula and descend into Hecate Cove, just west of the community of Quatsino. Side Bay, just east of Lawn Point, looks like it should be a good place to hide from northwest winds, but when the winds hit the coast they pass over the peninsula and into the bay. The presence or absence of trees over the hilltops influences where winds come down to the water.

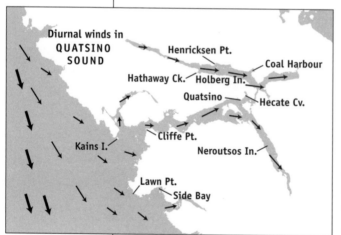

Fog moves into Quatsino Sound with westerly winds and can sock everything in. If it clears with daytime heating the diurnal inflow winds will soon follow. The diurnal inflow winds start near Cliffe Point and move into Quatsino Sound. On a hot sunny day they can howl even though there are no winds outside the sound. Sometimes the winds will turn down into Neroutsos Inlet. When the inflow winds are strong, there will be no winds in Holberg Inlet. Occasionally when Holberg develops its own sea breeze westerly wind, they will begin near Hathaway Creek and blow toward Coal Harbour. Outflow north-easterly winds develop overnight after the inflow has stopped and continue into the morning hours.

Brooks Peninsula

The orientation of westerly winds around Brooks Peninsula changes with the pressure-slope. The winds hit right along the coast when the pressure-slope is southwesterly, but as it turns toward the west the winds tend to head almost due south, so the centre of the plume becomes progressively farther away from the coast the farther toward the northwest the pressure-slope becomes. In this case the northwest winds impact Brooks Peninsula and through corner effects create winds that are two or three times stronger than they were before encountering the peninsula. A 10 to 15 knot northwest wind north of the peninsula becomes a 30 to 35 knot wind near Solander Island. Even halfway across Brooks Bay toward Klaskish Inlet the winds are much reduced.

The plume of winds extends south from Cape Cook, leaving the area inside Clerke Point with light winds. The difficulty is that occasionally, when the conditions are right, the northwest winds will pass over the peninsula and plunge down onto the water on the south side. This happens only when there is an inversion in the atmosphere just above the top of the peninsula. If the height of this inversion is much higher than

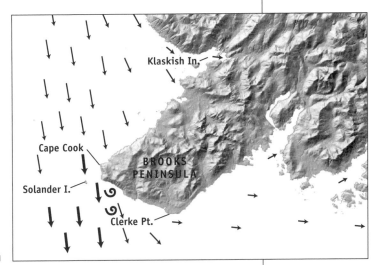

the top of the peninsula the winds will go aloft and will remain aloft so the air will be quiet at the water surface. Unfortunately there is no simple way to advise of the height of the inversion, so use the south side of the Brooks for shelter with caution. Occasionally small waterspouts will form on the south side of the peninsula but they are not as severe as the ones that form on the north side with southeast winds.

Mariners have a number of sayings about weather based on what is seen on and around Brooks Peninsula. One of these sayings is that "if the weather has been nice for several days and you see Solander Island looking like a pillar, and sometimes upside down, then you know that in a day or two you will get strong southeast winds." Another says that "when Cape Cook has its 'cap on' or when the 'woolly worms' are seen on Brooks Peninsula it is a sure sign that hard westerlies will hit before the day is out." The "woolly worms" are so called because the cap cloud that forms on top of Brooks Peninsula has caterpillar legs that extend out into each valley right to the end of the cape.

West Vancouver Island

EASTERLY PRESSURE-SLOPE WINDS

Southeast winds affecting western Vancouver Island during the autumn and winter occur ahead of approaching fronts. Depending on the orientation of the fronts the winds will affect some areas more than others. In most cases when the front approaches from the west or northwest the strongest winds will be at the northern end of Vancouver Island and will be weaker farther south, especially south of Estevan Point, which is often a dividing point for weather. When the front approaches from the southwest, the southeast winds don't enter any of the inlets, and the strongest winds are found offshore and near the headlands of the Hesquiat and Brooks peninsulas. The inlets will experience light northeast winds.

Brooks Peninsula to Estevan Point

Kyuquot and Yuquot in the local native tongue, both mean winds that come from all directions. Within the inside water the winds change significantly with a slight change of wind direction. When the pressure-slope is east or northeast there may be storm force southeast winds outside but there will be little wind inside. However, when the pressure-slope changes to southeast the winds move into the sound. The change is very subtle and doesn't appear to happen only when a front passes.

Brooks Pen. — Johnson L.
Crowther Ch.
Kyuquot — Union I.
Tahsish In.
BROOKS PENINSULA TO ESTEVAN POINT
Port Eliza — Esperanza In.
Catala I.
Yuquot
Hesquiat Pen.
Estevan Pt.

When the pressure-slope is northeasterly, the winds come out of Tahsish Inlet as an outflow wind. When the pressure-slope is easterly, the winds move parallel with the coast, passing the southern end of Crowther Channel but do not move into the channel. The easterly winds pass over Union Island and bounce off the mountain behind the community of Kyuquot and come down into the harbour. Winds also move into channels such as Port Eliza. Winds pile up against the mountains just west of the opening of Esperanza Inlet and create rough conditions as they funnel through the channel just north of Catala Island, which is quite appropriately named Rolling Roadstead.

Drill cores have been taken in the lake on Catala Island to research past tsunamis. Layers of sand and gravel found within peat deposits were linked to a tsunami that occurred on 26 January 1700. The tsumani was caused by the last great earthquake (magnitude 9) in the Cascadia subduction zone. Wave run-ups associated with such a tsunami have been estimated at five metres off the coast of Vancouver Island, and up to 15 to 20 metres at the heads of the inlets.

Southeast winds are enhanced as they pass around Estevan Point, but since the outer part of Hesquiat Peninsula is not mountainous like Brooks Peninsula, the enhancement is not as strong, nor are the downwind and lee effects as pronounced. There is some lee sheltering on the north side in most southeast wind events. Since the Estevan Point light station is on land, and not within the band of stronger winds that occur off the point, it does not report the same strength of winds as those offshore.

When the pressure-slope is southeast, which occurs close to the passage of the front, the winds blow into Kyuquot Channel, then between Union Island and Hohoae Island, and over to Chamiss Bay and Kashutl Inlet. They generally don't extend much east of the line from the western tip of Hohoae Island to western Moketas Island, and as a result are often calm through Markale Passage, except at the eastern end, which gets winds from Pinnace Channel.

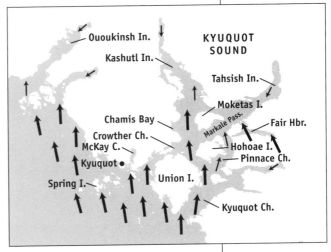

Fair Harbour can be quiet with most southeast wind events but when the winds offshore approach hurricane force, the winds come down over the mountains to the south, and hit hard onto the water. Winds of 100 knots have been observed in the harbour. Locals don't leave their boats tied up there in the winter. Cars parked at the head of the inlet have had windows damaged by rocks picked up by the winds or have been popped out. Fair Harbour can be anything but fair.

| SOUTH COAST | **WEST VANCOUVER ISLAND** |

With a southeasterly pressure-slope the winds move into Esperanza Inlet, and over the flats of Hesquiat Peninsula, and into Nootka Sound. Winds move up into Tahsis Inlet but generally do not blow with any great strength all the way up to the community of Tahsis. By the time the pressure-slope has turned far enough to the south to allow winds to enter the inlets, the front will normally be past, and the wind gradient will have dropped down considerably.

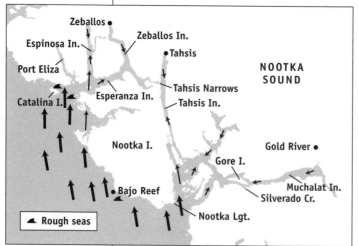

As a result the winds will be much less than those that occurred earlier outside the inlet. The time that they do get strong southerly winds is when the pressure-slope is near 120° and the air is stable, as it is in the warm sector between the warm and cold fronts.

The sea conditions can be locally bad, when southeast winds enter Nootka Sound and meet the remnants of the outgoing northeast winds. Only when there are rapid pressure rises behind the front will there be really strong winds moving into the inlets. Muchalat Inlet remains calm even with very strong southeasterlies offshore, except at the western end near Gore Island which gets some wind across Silverado Creek.

Zeballos Inlet is aligned northwest to southeast and so should be open to experiencing strong southeast winds. But because of the high mountains at both ends of the inlet, winds are not funnelled into the inlet from outside. The winds, as a result, are only created locally by the pressure difference across the inlet, so they rarely rise to extreme values. The winds are fetch limited, just like the seas in an inland waterway.

Seas and tidal currents are also enhanced near Estevan Point due to the shallowing of the water near the point, and can be dangerous. Tides are not that strong in most parts of the inlets except in narrow openings such as Tahsis Narrows. Huge swells can move across the shallow waters of Hesquiat Bar creating breaking waves that have damaged fishing boats. Swells that move into Nootka Sound are usually dissipated by the time they reach Strange Island.

Swell moves into Esperanza Inlet but becomes weak as it moves up Zeballos Inlet. Most swells come from the west or northwest. Tides are generally not a problem in the Kyuquot and Nootka sounds except through narrow openings, such as those that lead into McKay Cove, Johnson Lagoon (south of Brooks Peninsula), and Tahsis Narrows. The reefs just outside Esperanza Inlet are very rough with southeast winds against the tides. Bajo Reef is also bad.

> During the Alaska tsunami event in 1964 the water came up Esperanza Inlet and into Zeballos Inlet, and picked up the community hall and a few houses. There was more damage done in Zeballos per capita than in Port Alberni.

Clayoquot and Barkley sounds

Clayoquot and Barkley sounds respond to southeast winds in a similar way to Nootka Sound in that the inner waters don't get the full force of the winds until the pressure-slope turns more to the southeast. The front and associated winds tend to weaken somewhat south of Estevan Point. Southeast winds hitting the outer edge of the coast blow straight into Schooner Cove. One small section of the cove has logs that have been thrown more than 20 metres above the normal winter high water line. Ahous Bay offers some shelter from southeast winds when close to the beach, while the winds will howl just outside the bay, near Foam Reefs.

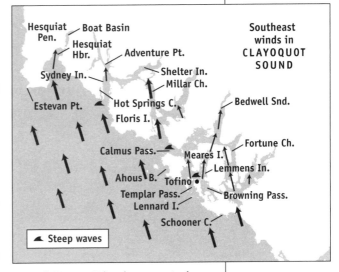

Southeast winds move up Millar Channel, and are squally over the top of Floris Island, at the western part of Shelter Inlet. They blow up Fortune Channel and into Lemmens Inlet, and after crossing the top of Meares Island are gusty in Bedwell Sound. Browning Pass and Templar Channel have similar strength southeast winds.

SOUTH COAST | **WEST VANCOUVER ISLAND**

Southeast winds against an ebbing tide create dangerous steep waves over Coomes Bank in Calmus Passage, near the mouth of Hot Springs Cove, and near the mouth of Lemmens Inlet. Giant swells move across Hesquiat Bar and into Hesquiat Harbour, where they have damaged fishing boats, but Boat Basin at the head of the harbour is a good anchorage. Seas also spread up along Floris Island and into Sydney Inlet but usually end before Adventure Point.

On 12 October 1998 a deep low moved up toward the Queen Charlotte Islands. The front crossed the Barkley Sound area in the morning. Winds at Solander Island rose to 58 knots with gusts to 69, yet they only rose to 35 knots at Lennard Island. But with this seemingly innocuous system, 1 to 2 acres of old-growth cedars with diameters more than two metres were blown down in a twister-like downdraft.

Barkley Sound is the most open of the sounds on the west side of Vancouver Island. All the other sounds have a few large islands with only narrow channels between them. Barkley Sound, in contrast, has many small islands that lie in near-straight lines running parallel with the northwest and southeast edges to the sound. The waterways between these island chains are much wider and more open, and as a result Barkley Sound has different types of wind and sea effects.

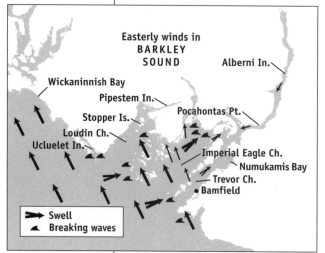

Easterly winds in **BARKLEY SOUND**

Alberni In.
Wickaninnish Bay
Pipestem In.
Stopper Is.
Pocahontas Pt.
Loudin Ch.
Ucluelet In.
Imperial Eagle Ch.
Numukamis Bay
Trevor Ch.
Bamfield

➤ Swell
▲ Breaking waves

When the pressure-slope is easterly the southeast winds flow parallel with Vancouver Island across the mouth of Barkley Sound. When it tilts a little toward the southeast the winds will sweep across the southwest corner of the sound. Loudoun Channel is hit harder than Imperial Eagle Channel, which is protected by the mountains behind Cape Beale and Bamfield. When the pressure-slope is closer to southeast the winds spread up Trevor Channel to just beyond Bamfield to join with some coming down the mountains, and across Numukamis Bay. They move up to hit the Stopper Islands, but remain calm just beyond, in Pipestem Inlet. Only when the pressure-slope becomes more southerly will the winds blow all the way into the sound and up

Alberni Inlet to near Pocahontas Point. As a result of these variations there are times when southeast winds are very strong outside of the sound but light inside, and other times when it blows hard inside as well as outside. But the fact that not all inside sections of Barkley Sound get strong southeast wind, does not prevent them from getting their full share of rain.

> On September 1997 a low stalled offshore but sent 9 to 12 metre swells out ahead of it. Three people were swept into the water at Wickaninnish Bay. Many people have been plucked off the rocks by huge waves crashing onto the coast. Glass balls thrown up by waves have been found in the forest well beyond the sandy beaches. People have been soaked by water some 15 metres up in the forests.

Swells can roll into Barkley Sound at any time, irrespective of the speed and direction of the winds. The swells shorten and increase in height as they cross the shallow waters near the outer islands, and at the head of the various channels. The swells also change direction after interacting with the bottom topography. The seas break right across the mouth of Ucluelet Inlet. Imperial Eagle Channel has been described as a bowling alley with swells rolling from the front, where they are long and rounded, to the back, where they are compressed into short steep waves with breaking tops. Swells of 1½ - 2 metres are not uncommon. The waves cross behind the single islands, but the larger islands and those that are in groups offer shelter from the incoming swells.

The wind reports from Estevan Point are a reference for the outside waters, while stations such as Nootka and Quatsino are indicators of conditions in the inlets.

NORTHERLY PRESSURE-SLOPE WINDS

Brooks Peninsula to Estevan Point

In winter when there is strong outflow in mainland inlets the winds pass over Vancouver Island and funnel through its inlets. They can reach speeds of 30 to 35 knots, but in most instances will be lower. The radar wind image of 6 February 2000 in Chapter 3 shows outflow winds passing down Tahsish Inlet and out through Crowther Inlet. Kashutl Inlet does not get strong outflow winds. Strong turbulent outflow also moves out of Ououkinsh Inlet. A similar plume of winds, which likely reached speeds of 30 knots, moved down Muchalat Inlet and extended some 10 miles beyond the mouth of Nootka Sound, while the Nootka lighthouse only reported 14 knots. The community of Gold River doesn't get strong outflow winds.

Tatchu Point is the official boundary point between the marine forecast regions of West Coast Vancouver Island North and West Coast Vancouver Island South. It was a compromise position as the original thought was to divide the island into three parts with Brooks Peninsula and Estevan Point being the dividing points.

If an arctic outflow continues for several days with temperatures well below freezing, the fresh water at the head of the inlets will freeze. The top of Zeballos Inlet, for instance, will freeze to produce a centimetre of ice. The freezing will spread down to the twin islands at the bend of the inlet opposite the mouth of Little Zeballos River. The water near the outlets of other rivers, even when not at the head of inlets, will also freeze over in colder years. Kendrick Inlet, into which flows Kendrick River, had three to five cm of ice one year. In most cases only a skin of ice forms, which larger boats easily break through.

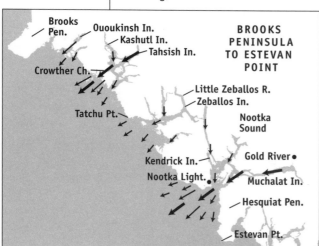

Generally the period of cold weather doesn't last much more than a week. Nootka light station had 12 years between 1978 and 2001 in which the temperatures dipped below -2°C. There were only five years that had temperatures below -5°C, with the coldest report of -10°C on 2 February 1989. Tahsis village, at the head of the inlet, recorded temperatures below -5°C in 10 out of 15 years of record between 1981 and 2001. Nootka gets on average about 15 cm of snow per year, while Gold River, just a short distance up the Muchalat Inlet and farther inland, gets 120-150 cm. Freezing spray is not commonly observed in the inlets.

Clayoquot and Barkley Sounds

Bedwell Sound and Herbert Inlet receive most of the northerly outflow winds that occur in Clayoquot Sound, though it is usually much less than the winds that come out of Barkley Sound. The outflow from Bedwell Sound crosses over the top of Meares Island and through Lemmens Inlet before hitting Tofino, which is usually does once or twice a year. Northerly winds are most common in December and January but also occur in mid-November. The calmest conditions at Long Beach occur during outflow conditions when there are no lows offshore.

Barkley Sound experiences the strongest outflow winds of southern Vancouver Island. The winds pass out through Alberni Inlet, and when the pressure-slope is northeasterly, flow through Imperial Eagle Channel and over the Broken Group islands near the mouth of Barkley Sound. Coaster Channel often gets a large part of this wind. When the pressure-slope is more northerly the winds will pour through Trevor Channel before exiting the sound. In this instance Bamfield will get some of the northerly winds. In either case almost all of Barley Sound is affected except for the northwest corner beyond Peacock Channel. The plume of winds extends well beyond the mouth of

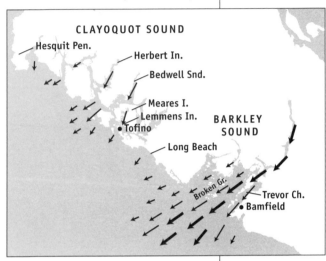

the sound and bends northward if the winds offshore are easterly, which they often are because of the outflow from Juan de Fuca Strait.

In a typical winter heavy wet snow begins when there are still light northeast winds in the inlets but southeast winds are blowing offshore. A quick dump of 2 or 3 cm falls in a half hour or so, then an hour later it warms up and is all gone. Bigger snowfalls, which stay longer, happen with northerly outflow winds. In years past significant snowfalls occurred several times each winter. A snow storm that lasts through the night may happen once every five years. It hails in the Tofino area more than it snows. Lightning and hail occur more frequently from November to March than during the summer months. They seem to be most frequent at night. They are associated with cold air behind active frontal systems that develops cumulonimbus cloud cells. Storm damage from these storms is localized, and not usually significant.

SOUTHERLY PRESSURE-SLOPE WINDS

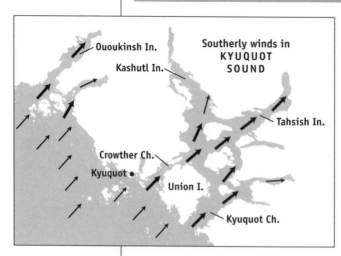

Southerly winds in
**KYUQUOT
SOUND**

Kyuquot Sound

Many of the channels of Kyuquot Sound are open to the southwest so they experience the full thrust of southwest winds. The winds increase in speed as they funnel through Crowther and Kyuquot channels before they move into Tahsish Inlet. The western entrance to Kyuquot is open to southwest winds. Thunder and heavy hail accompanying these winds can come in waves, turning the cove white.

Nootka Sound

In Nootka Sound southwest winds blow through Nuchatlitz Inlet, across the peninsula on Nootka Island, and out Blowhole Bay into Tahsis Inlet. They also pass through Zuciarte Channel and into Muchalat Inlet. Winds in the inlets that run toward the north or northeast, such as Port Eliza, Espinosa, and Tahsis Inlets, remain light. Some southwesterly winds work a little way up Zeballos Inlet but do not normally make it all the way up to the community of Zeballos.

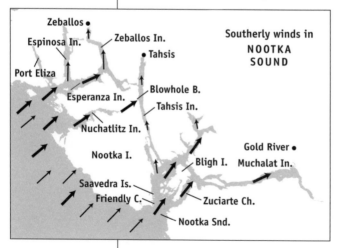

Southerly winds in
**NOOTKA
SOUND**

Fog often spreads into Nootka Sound with southerly winds, and fills almost all of the waterways around Bligh Island but does not usually spread very far up Tahsis Inlet. Due to the orientation of the southerly flow the fog often passes over Friendly Cove at the Nootka light station but leaves the area west of the Saavedra Islands wide open.

The sequence of weather systems that is referred to as the "pineapple express" gives a period of nearly non-stop rain to the south coast. This pattern develops when a front extends to the southwest of Vancouver Island, with a series of frontal waves and lows that develop along it and repeatedly cross the coast.

Clayoquot and Barkley sounds

The typical frontal passage sees strong southeast winds ahead of the front followed by much lighter south to southwest winds behind it. The only time that southerly winds are really strong is when the pressure rises sharply behind the front. This usually occurs with a strong front or with the passage of a coastal low over Vancouver Island. Only the strongest southerly winds are notable, even if they are very brief.

The worst winter conditions are often not with southeast or southerly winds but with the strong westerly winds that occur behind the fronts. A case to illustrate this point occurred during the early morning of 11 November 1983. The wind at Estevan Point ahead of the front was southeast 54 knots but when the southwest winds behind the front poured across Tofino Harbour the gusts rose to nearly 110 knots. A houseboat was blown off its foundation and overturned. Another house off McCall Island in Tofino Inlet imploded. Southwest winds have been seen to funnel through Browning Passage, rising from 30 to 35 knots at the entrance to 50 to 60 knots with gusts to 80 near Indian Island.

An interesting phenomenon develops as a flooding tide moves around both sides of Wickaninnish Island. A series of standing waves stretching some 30 metres form over the sandbar between Wickaninnish and Stubbs islands. These waves form what is locally called a "zipper." It happens most often in spring.

When the pressure-slope is from the south or southeast, southerly winds pour up through Maurus Channel, and after impacting Lone Cone Mountain the winds come down hard onto the water near Robert Point. The winds can be strong enough to lay a fishing boat on its side. Eddies and waterspouts form off the point. On several occasions a string of 15 or 20 waterspouts were observed extending from Robert Point toward Kraan Head. They were about 15 to 20 metres high, 10 to 15 metres in diameter, and spaced about 25 metres apart. The waterspouts formed when the winds coming up the channel

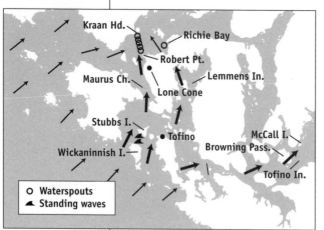

Kraan Hd.
Richie Bay
Robert Pt.
Maurus Ch.
Lemmens In.
Lone Cone
Stubbs I.
Tofino
McCall I.
Wickaninnish I.
Browning Pass.
Tofino In.

○ Waterspouts
▲ Standing waves

were at least 40 knots. Waterspouts have also been seen in Ritchie Bay. They likely formed in the convergence of the winds from Maurus Channel and those coming up Lemmens Inlet, on the east side of Lone Cone Mountain.

Southwest winds move into Barkley Sound and extend at least partway up Alberni Inlet. The area off Bamfield gets some wind at this time. These winds are brief, and may be accompanied by thunder and lightning. Waterspouts are not uncommon in the unstable air that frequently accompanies southerly winds.

Debris tends to accumulate in Deadman Cove, a little bay just east of Cape Beale. Many things, including bodies of drowned people, have been washed in there. The waters between Pachena Point and Cape Beale always seems to be

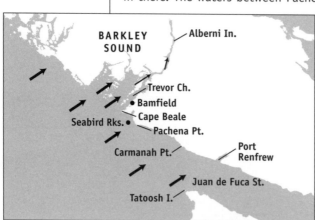

BARKLEY
SOUND
Alberni In.
Trevor Ch.
Bamfield
Cape Beale
Seabird Rks.
Pachena Pt.
Carmanah Pt.
Port Renfrew
Juan de Fuca St.
Tatoosh I.

rough, but are especially bad with southwest winds near Seabird Rocks, and just off Cape Beale. An outgoing tide through Trevor Channel will break just west of Cape Beale when it encounters strong westerly swell. Fog is pushed into Barkley Sound with south to southwest winds.

The mouth of Juan de Fuca Strait has been called the Graveyard of the Pacific because of the number of vessels that got into trouble or sank in this area during the days of sail. Between 1830 and 1927 there were 137 shipping tragedies in this area. The West Coast trail was established along 44 miles of coastline between Port Renfrew and Bamfield in order to assist shipwrecked survivors. Prior to this trail any survivors were taken by canoe to Fort Victoria by local First Nations people.

WESTERLY PRESSURE-SLOPE WINDS

During a quiet day between April and mid-September, with no major systems approaching the coast, all inlets get a light outflow at night and in the early morning, with inflow winds during the afternoon. The inflow starts near 1000 and increases until around 1700 hours, then dies away with the setting sun. The winds tend to be light near the mouths of the inlets, and increase to 20 to 25 knots toward the head. The hotter it gets the stronger the winds will be. If the winds rise quickly they will drop equally quickly. The strength of the winds is connected to the difference in temperature between land and sea. The greater the contrast in the temperature the greater the winds. If fog is present in the morning the diurnal inflow winds don't begin until after the fog has cleared. The northerly outflow overnight is strongest in spring and early summer when snow remains on the mountaintops.

Diurnal fog

Fog is a frequent problem west of Vancouver Island. It occurs most frequently south of Estevan Point, and is worst close to the mouth of Juan de Fuca Strait. The cold waters in this area maintain an almost constant fog through July and August, and into early September. During El Niño years, when water temperatures are higher than normal, fog tends to be less frequent.

> It has been said that when Tofino gets temperatures less than 20°C then no fog will form. It also doesn't form when the water temperature rises to near 18°C, as may happen in an El Niño year.

There are two basic types of advection fog. The most common one occurs simply because of the temperature difference between air and water. It thins or thickens according to daytime heating and cooling, and as a result can be called a diurnal fog. The winds are generally light but sun-induced inflow winds strengthen once the fog lifts. The other type is related to what is called a stratus surge.

Diurnal fog, as the name suggests, has a diurnal cycle of change. When the pressure-slope is northwesterly the strong northwest winds remain offshore, and do not collapse onto the coast in the afternoon. Light winds remain along the southwestern coast, and a bank of fog lies five miles or so offshore. Often there will be a period of two or three days when this pattern continues, and sunny skies prevail. The temperatures will slowly rise each day until temperatures reach the mid-to upper twenties over land. With this heating the pressure-slope backs a bit and the northwest winds move toward the coast, and the fog follows. Once the fog reaches the coast it normally remains for several days, though undergoing its daily cycle of change.

> In general terms it can be said that the air temperature must be high for fog to form, but in technical terms it is not the temperature of the air that is important but the difference between the temperature and dew point. The dew point is the temperature at which the air becomes saturated.

Typically fog moves onto the coast overnight, towards dawn. It begins to burn off near the land around 1000 to 1100 hours, and may clear completely by early afternoon. The fog retreats to a few miles offshore but it remains clear on the coast until the evening, when the cycle begins again. If the fog hasn't arrived by dawn it will come in around 0630 to 0700 hours, and does not begin to clear until around 1300 hours. If high cloud moves across the region it will slow the rate of daytime heating, and hence delay the time when the fog lifts. If thicker cloud moves in above the fog then the fog may not burn off at all. If the fog does not clear by midday then the amount of daytime heating will be less and the fog will roll in again earlier in the evening.

The fog generally spreads up the inlets with a wedge-like front, but sometimes it just gently appears as temperatures fall in the evening. Clearing begins near the head of the inlet, or near open fields and recently logged areas, as the open land heats up faster. You can watch fog react to heating over the land. Fog moving toward the coast may stop and burn off as it moves inland. The temperature difference between foggy areas and the warmer land creates strong sea breeze effects, and strengthens the inflow winds in the inlets. If there is fog offshore in the morning stronger inflow winds develop in the afternoon.

> It was suggested that you can tell something about how soon fog will come, and how bad it will be by its colour. White fog is very dense. The way fog lays on the horizon, and what clouds are on the local mountains are also signs to watch.

Stratus surge

The other type of advection fog is linked to the movement of a wave in the atmosphere that develops along the California coast, and moves northward up the Oregon and Washington coasts to the west coast of Vancouver Island. This travelling wave is called a stratus surge, for it is made visible by the fog and low stratus clouds that accompany it. The stratus and fog move with speeds typically near 15 knots but may at times rise to 30 knots. The onset of the fog is accompanied by a sudden increase of winds from light up to southeast 25 to 30 knots.

When these winds round Brooks Peninsula they often rise to gale force. Northwest winds remain well offshore as the southeast winds pour up along the coast. A stratus surge normally happens after a period of hot sunny weather and is usually accompanied by an onshore push of winds into Juan de Fuca Strait. The stratus surge often arrives on the west coast of Vancouver Island overnight, or in the early morning hours.

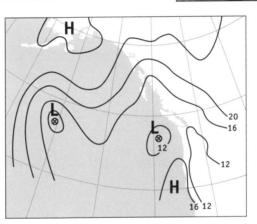

Satellite picture for 2300 hours 13 June 2002, and a weather map for one hour later.

←

Kyuquot Sound

When an offshore ridge of high pressure creates a west or northwest pressure-slope, the northwest winds remain off the coast during the overnight and morning hours, and collapse toward the coast during the afternoon. As a result of this summer pattern, many mariners try to go well around Estevan Point in the morning, before the winds increase.

When strong northwest winds are offshore, the inlets have light outflow winds. The winds remain light all the way out to Rugged Point. It is only when the pressure-slope becomes more southwesterly that the westerly winds enter the inlets. They will then blow through Crowther Channel and into Tahsish Inlet. They will also pass through Kyuquot Channel into Amai Inlet.

regional weather guides

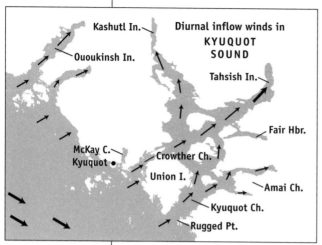

Kyuquot Sound will have diurnal inflow and outflow winds during a sunny summer day. The inflow winds develop in all the inlets but are strongest in Kashutl and Tahsish Inlets. The outflow comes primarily down Tashish Inlet. During a period of hot weather Kyuquot will get outflow winds in the early morning, which come down through McKay Cove. Fair Harbour remains quiet.

Nootka Sound

In Nootka Sound the offshore-ridge westerly winds blow into Nuchatlitz Inlet and over the peninsula, and out Blowhole Bay. Vessels passing the Blowhole slow down in anticipation of getting sudden, strong side winds. Rough seas

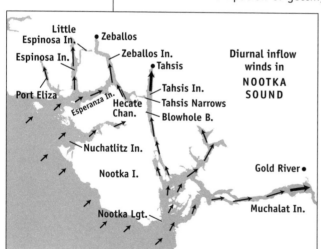

develop over the reefs just outside Esperanza Inlet when westerly winds blow against an outgoing tide. The Nootka lighthouse, which is just inside the sound, generally gets much less wind than outside.

The diurnal westerly winds howl up Muchalat (sometimes locally called Miserable Inlet) giving short, sharp chop. They reach their peak around 1730 hours then drop off quickly with the setting sun. Inflow winds do go up the valley from the harbour of Gold River but only extend as far as the golf course, just south of the Gold River community itself. Gold River gets a northerly wind during the hot summer days. Esperanza has a strong afternoon inflow, which is worst near the junction with Hecate Channel, where it combines with the inflow up Zeballos Inlet. Tahsis also draws up a strong inflow wind, but Tahsis Narrows has little wind. Port Eliza and Espinosa Inlet draw up enough inflow to create choppy seas, with Espinosa being the stronger of the two. Nuchatlitz doesn't have a strong inflow.

> Zeballos, which gets about 4000mm of rain a year, celebrates their rainfall during an Umbrella Festival in August. The terms "horizontal rain" and "frog stranglers" are sometimes used by the locals to describe the heavy rain and strong winds.

Zeballos gets some fog that crosses over the peninsula between it and Little Espinosa Inlet. Zeballos tends to get more fog than Tahsis Inlet, which gets more than Muchalat Inlet. Nootka Sound will often get more periods of lowered visibilities in fog and rain during the winter months between November and January, than it gets during the summer.

> If a cap cloud forms over Kavok Mountain, north of Zeballos, you know that fog is coming.

Clayoquot Sound

The outer coastline is fully exposed to northwest winds when they come onto the coast. The winds will move into all channels that open to the west.

Westerly winds blow as a solid wind into Shelter Inlet. They pass above Meares Island and into Bedwell Sound, where a few years ago they were strong enough to destroy a fish farm. A 20 knot westerly wind offshore increases as it passes through Browning Passage so that it rises to 40 knots after crossing the peninsula into Windy Bay. The winds will be calm, just to the north, in Fortune Channel. The channel between Vargas Island and Meares Island is also protected from westerly winds.

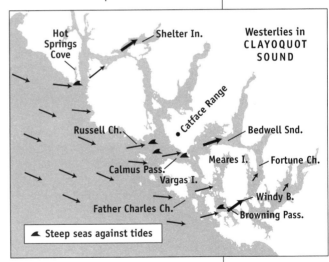

Tidal currents in Clayoquot Sound are a little stronger than in Barkley Sound. As a result, westerly winds blowing against an outflowing ebb tide can create dangerous seas. The areas that are bad are localized but include: just outside Hot Springs Cove, Russell Channel, off Catface Range in Calmus Passage, Father Charles Channel, and in Browning Passage.

SOUTH COAST | **WEST VANCOUVER ISLAND**

Barkley Sound

Alberni Inlet goes through the typical cycle of light winds in the morning with increasing southerly winds from late morning through the afternoon. The seas

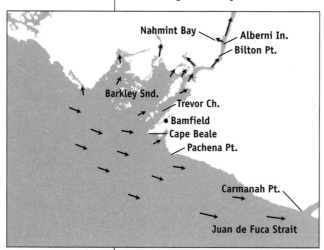

don't get too high because of the bends of the inlet. Alberni Inlet does not get much northerly wind overnight. Nahmint Bay draws up inflow winds during a hot summer day, and has colder outflow winds in winter and early spring. Trevor Channel is pretty quiet in summer. Barkley Sound is more affected by swells than Clayoquot Sound because it is more open, with fewer islands to break them up. There are few places to hide, as the swells move right to the back of the sound.

When fog moves into Barkley Sound it spreads almost everywhere, but is especially thick in Trevor Channel, and off Bamfield. It spreads up Alberni Inlet, but usually stops near Bilton Point, some 15 miles south of Port Alberni. Barkley Sound, being closer to the pool of cold waters off the mouth of Juan de Fuca Strait, tends to get more fog than the other sounds farther north. Locations near the mouth of Juan de Fuca Strait, such as Cape Beale, Pachena Point, and Carmanah Point, all get extensive fog during the summer.

> During the winter months swell will move almost to the back of the sound. In Trevor Channel it doesn't normally go much beyond San Jose Islets. On 2 January 1992 a man who had been sitting watching the waves was swept off the rock as he got up to go. The wave climbed some six metres farther up the rock than previous ones.

North Coast

The North Coast, for the purposes of this book, consists of the entire area from Cape Caution to Dixon Entrance. It has been divided into three regions: **Open waters** *including Dixon Entrance, Hecate Strait, Queen Charlotte Sound, and the offshore areas; the* **Queen Charlotte Islands***; and the* **Northern mainland coast***.*

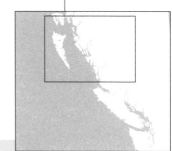

Cape Caution, which may appear to be a point like any other point, is one that lives up to its name. It stands at the threshold between the north and south coasts, like a guardian that invites you to pass and see the wonders of the north coast, but at the same time warns of the need to be prepared. Roderick Frazier Nash in an essay in the book *Exploring the North Coast of British Columbia* said that rounding Cape Caution "is a nautical coming of age" and those who make it this far enter "a fraternity of mutual respect where they experience the space, the solitude, and the silence of one of the world's wildest coastlines."

Open waters

Winds in the open, offshore waters can come from any direction. They are not constrained by topographical controls. The position of any nearby high or low pressure areas is what determines the direction of the wind. In the coastal inlets, on the other hand, the winds are strongly directed by topography to blow along the channels, as either inflow or outflow. Most of the coast lies between these two extremes, with a number of preferred wind directions.

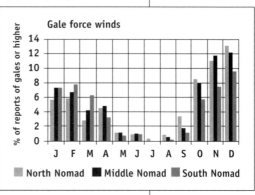

The graph shows the frequency of gales at the off-shore buoys (see following map for their locations) throughout the year. Gales are most frequent from October to December, and are least common from May though September. The transition to higher winds normally happens in late September. On average the highest wave heights occur in December, while the lowest values are in July and August. Note that the frequency of gales is higher at the south nomad buoy than at the other buoys in January, February, and March, but gales are less frequent from September through December. This is because the track of the lows is typically farther north in autumn, and farther south in winter.

NORTH COAST | **OPEN WATERS**

> The offshore marine forecast areas are named after the Bowie and Explorer seamounts. The Bowie seamount, 180km west of the Queen Charlotte Islands, is one of the shallowest seamounts in the northeast Pacific: its peak is just 25m below the water surface. The seamounts create an oasis of life in the mid-ocean desert. They are refuges for certain species of fish and a variety of unique plant and animal communities.

The maps show the average values of wave heights from the buoy network for December and July, and give estimated values for locations between the buoys. The average seas are lower close the mainland coast, and are least in the shadow of the outer islands. On the other coast note that the seas are lowest southwest of Vancouver Island.

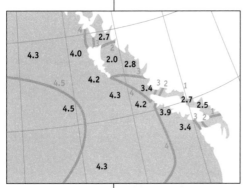

DECEMBER

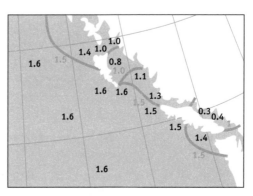

JULY

Waves

> The significant wave is defined as the average height of the highest 1/3 of all the waves. It approximates what an observer at sea would likely report.

The highest significant wave height recorded by Environment Canada on the coast is 14.9m. This occurred at the South Hecate buoy. Extreme waves are about twice the height of the significant wave. The highest recorded extreme waves are over 30m (100 feet) recorded at both the South Hecate buoy and the East Delwood buoy. A 30 metre wave was also recorded by the drilling rig *Sedco 135F* working in Queen Charlotte Sound, south of Cape St. James, on 22 October 1968. While these waves are huge, the more dangerous aspect is the rate that they can build from almost nothing to frightening heights. In the 1968 case the seas rose from three metres to 18 metres in just eight hours.

Northwesterly swell from offshore storms spreads into Queen Charlotte Sound and Dixon Entrance, but not into Hecate Strait. Westerly swells refract a little around Cape St. James, and affect the southern parts of Hecate Strait. Swell from the southwest or south spreads much farther up into Hecate Strait, only leaving the northwestern parts unaffected. Westerly swell passing into Dixon Entrance fans out as it passes Rose Spit, and moves as far south as Porcher Island. The height of the waves along the mainland coast is much less than Dixon Entrance. On the whole the northern section of Hecate Strait has much lower seas than the south.

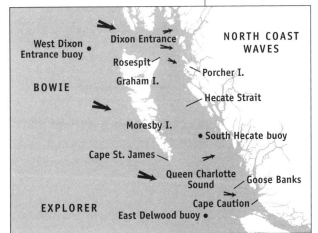

EASTERLY PRESSURE-SLOPE WINDS

Dixon Entrance

When the pressure-slope is at the northeast end of the easterly range the winds through Dixon Entrance will be easterly, but as the pressure-slope turns toward the southeast the winds change. The southeast winds from Hecate Strait will then pour over the shallow land of Rose Spit to affect the eastern end of Dixon Entrance. Southeast winds also move up the western side of Graham Island, but the middle area of Dixon Entrance will have lighter winds, especially in the south, close to Graham Island. The radar wind image of 13 October 2002 (Chapter 3) shows this quite well. The winds ease throughout Dixon Entrance if the pressure-slope rotates south of 130°.

> The Central Dixon buoy (like all other buoys) sits low in the water, and as a result does not record the full strength of winds that might be recorded by a passing ship. It will record, for example, 18 to 20 knots when Rose Spit is 25 to 30 knots.

Hecate Strait

Hecate Strait is a dangerous body of water, not just because of the severity of the winds but because of the rapidity with which the winds change. Winds can go from calm to insanely strong in an incredibly short time. One mariner cited an example when the winds in Hecate rose from almost nothing to 60 knots in half an hour.

In Hecate Strait there seem to be three categories of sea heights in most winter storms. The weakest one occurs when the front passes quickly, and the seas barely rise to 2 to 3 metres. The second is most common, with events that give gale to marginal storm force winds (40 to 50 knots). In this case five metre seas are produced, at least over southern sections of Hecate Strait and in Queen Charlotte Sound. The last category is produced when the strongest storms generate waves of over eight metres either from particularly strong southeast winds, or a very long fetch. Weather maps in this case would have isobars that extend in straight lines well south past northern Vancouver Island.

Queen Charlotte Sound

Queen Charlotte Sound is a large open body of water. Within it, three unique topographical features affect its winds and waves. The most apparent are northern Vancouver Island and southern Moresby Island. Both, with certain wind directions, steer bands of strong winds partway across the sound, or provide a little shelter from winds from other directions. The tidal currents at the southern end of the Queen Charlotte Islands, near Cape St. James are particularly strong and complex, and have a significant effect against seas, especially from the south and southwest.

The other topographic feature, the shape of the seabed, is not as apparent. The three troughs that extend across the ocean floor, with two ridges between them, are thought to influence the height of some of the longer swell waves that move across the sound by causing a converging of the waves around the ridges, thereby causing increased sea heights. Some of the highest sea heights reported on the BC coast have occurred over Queen Charlotte Sound, and the bathymetry of the ocean floor may have boosted these values to some degree.

> Remember that with a seven metre (24 feet) tidal range the currents may be very strong, and when winds are against these currents, conditions may be dangerous.

Queen Charlotte Sound is often the preferred location for the passage of coastal lows. When lows develop close to the coast they will frequently move from the southwest across Queen Charlotte Sound, before weakening over the

Hecate was a Greek goddess that had three heads, which allowed her to look in three directions at once, and hence was called the goddess of the crossroads. Hecate Strait lies between three waterways: Dixon Entrance, Queen Charlotte Sound, and the inlets of the mainland coast.

Coast Mountains. As a result the winds can be extremely strong over southern sections of the sound while parts in the north will get off with much lighter northerly winds.

Over the open waters of the central coast it takes two or three days after a big storm for the swell to subside. Goose Banks are shallow, allowing the seas to peak up, making it quite dangerous. The dominant wind north of Cape Caution is northeast while to the south it is southeast. Cape Caution, as its name aptly suggests, requires caution when passing it, for winds from southeast and northwest can be particularly strong.

NORTHERLY PRESSURE-SLOPE WINDS

When the pressure-slope is northerly the winds are primarily limited to coming out of the coastal inlets. Dixon Entrance can get much of the wind from the Portland Inlet. These plumes of strong winds, as the radar wind image of 15 April 2001 in Chapter 3 shows, create a general area of choppy seas along the east coast of the Charlottes. Only as the pressure-slope becomes more northerly do bands of stronger winds exit from the inlets of the Alaska Panhandle. When the pressure-slope turns into the range of easterlies (060° to 130°) then the outflow winds through the inlets ease and the southeast winds in Hecate Strait increase. If the pressure-slope were to back from the north into the westerly range then northwest winds would begin to strengthen along the mainland coast. In general, a northerly pressure-slope produces quite good conditions in Hecate Strait.

> It takes some 12 or 16 hours (at 4-6 knots) to cross from the Queen Charlotte Islands to the mainland coast.

Queen Charlotte Sound also gets winds that exit from the inlets of the Central Coast and from Queen Charlotte Strait. These winds raise the seas, but normally not to a level of major concern. The southern part of the sound will be affected by strong arctic outflow winds exiting the inlets of the mainland coast. In most outflow events, however, the sound is more affected by the proximity of lows or fronts that may be lurking just outside the area than by the outflow itself.

West of the Charlottes the outflow winds consist primarily of jets moving out of the inlets with calm areas between. Like Queen Charlotte Sound it is affected by weather systems that lie to the west of the coast giving it strengthened easterly winds and more cloud.

SOUTHERLY PRESSURE-SLOPE WINDS

The radar wind images in the previous chapter show the south to southwest winds spreading across the region. Remember that southerly winds are a transition wind, and as a result are normally short lived, and can change to either easterly or westerly winds with a very slight change of the pressure-slope. As the pressure-slope veers toward the west the winds in Dixon Entrance become westerly, and pour directly across to Dundas I. and the mainland coast. If the pressure-slope backs into the east then southeast winds spread up Hecate Strait, and across Rose Spit into Dixon Entrance. Out in the open waters of Queen Charlotte Sound the winds blow from the southwest without being turned to either the southeast or northwest by the topography.

> The shift from southeast to southwest is a major concern to mariners. The timing of this shift depends on the timing of the passage of the front. The mariners in Hecate Strait listen for wind shifts at Kindakun Rock and Langara I. to indicate the timing of shifts in Hecate. Cape St. James is used to indicate upcoming wind shifts for the Central Coast.

WESTERLY PRESSURE-SLOPE WINDS

The offshore-ridge westerly winds that pass over the open waters of Dixon Entrance, Hecate Strait, and Queen Charlotte Sound are most influenced by the orientation of the pressure-slope, and only to a lesser extent by diurnal effects. The diurnal effects that they do experience are most noticeable near the coastal edges, as the land heats up during the day more quickly than the ocean waters. Daytime heating draws the winds toward the land and into the channels near the edge of the open water. This landward bending of the winds takes place on both sides of the waterway with winds in the middle, well away from the land, continuing in the direction determined by the pressure-slope.

If the ridge causing the westerly winds is weak then there will be more noticeable diurnal heating effects, producing both strength and direction changes that extend farther out from the coast. If the ridge is strong then the westerly winds will blow steadily for days with no apparent weakening overnight, nor strengthening during the afternoon, nor tilting of the winds toward the land. Also, if it is cloudy, the diurnal effects don't occur.

> Fog is a problem across Queen Charlotte Sound in August, and continues, off and on, into October. The worst areas lie over western sections, near the edge of the continental shelf, and from northern Vancouver Island toward the mainland coast.

Diurnal heating is felt more strongly through the narrower channels of the Alaska Panhandle than in the more open Dixon Entrance. During a hot summer day, inflow winds in the panhandle counteract the northwesterlies in Dixon Entrance, causing them to be lighter, while at night the outflow tendency strengthens the northwest winds. Plumes of wind coming out from the Alaska Panhandle also create bands of higher seas.

When the pressure-slope is between southwest and west, winds from the west-northwest flow through Dixon Entrance, and strongly impact the north shore of Graham Island. They are particularly bad as they funnel south of Langara Island. The conditions are treacherous when the winds meet the strong tidal current flowing out of Masset Sound.

The seas, as well as westerly swell, sharpen up when against the ebbing tide. Westerly swell moving into Dixon Entrance peaks over the Learmonth Bank, where they create overfalls and rips. In most cases the westerly swells that pass through Dixon Entrance are cut in half by the time they reach Dundas Island, and with a flooding tide they are barely noticeable unless the winds have been blowing for several days. Westerly seas need to be more than four metres at the West Dixon Entrance buoy before much swell is noticed at Prince Rupert. The swells steepen when they counter ebbing tides from coastal inlets.

The highest natural liquid water temperature ever measured on earth, an amazing 372°C, has been recorded in the Endeavour hot vents (located about 130 nautical miles southwest of Cape Scott). The vents have unique life forms that may not be found anywhere else on earth.

Queen Charlotte Islands

The Queen Charlotte Islands, Haida Gwaii to its native inhabitants, consist of more than 150 islands, with a total area of 1,018,000 hectares. According to the 2001 census it has a population of about 5,000. The fascinating history and culture of the Haida people, the beauty and rugged nature of the land, and the remoteness are all part of the picture that lures more and more visitors to this area each year.

Barb Rowsell, of Anvil Cove Charters, made an interesting observation: "Before there was a national park on South Moresby people seemed to be in awe when we said that we ran boats on the Charlottes, but now, somehow, with it being a park everyone with a 10 foot car-topper feels qualified to set off."

Declaring South Moresby to be a national park has not tamed the elements!

EASTERLY PRESSURE-SLOPE WINDS

Some say that the winds at Rose Spit can be as fierce as those near Cape St. James, and that the winds near the spit may be even worse than what is reported from the observation site. Southeast winds spread across the peninsula, but are generally weaker and backed more into the east on the north side of the peninsula, in McIntyre Bay. The winds are often backed into the east across Dixon Entrance because northeasterly outflow from Portland Inlet continues until the front is almost past. Since southeast winds are coming off the land of the peninsula, the fetch is short and the seas are manageable. Naden Harbour and Masset Inlet get southeast winds when there are very strong southeast winds in Hecate, but they are not nearly as strong as at Rose Spit. Beware of the tidal currents north of Langara Island, near St. Margaret Point.

St. Margaret Pt.
Langara I.
Rose Spit
McIntyre B.
Naden Hbr.
GRAHAM I.
Tian Hd.
Hecate St.
Masset In.
Cape Ball
Overfalls
Steep seas

The Langara Island reporting site is sheltered from southeast winds, and so does not record the strength of winds that may be occurring a short distance offshore. It may report only 10 to 15 knots when winds are southeast 40-50 knots just to the west of the island. Langara Island, however, does give a good indication of northwest and northeast winds.

The shallowness of Hecate Strait near Graham Island causes the seas to steepen enough for the waves to break, and create "holes" in the sea. It is particularly bad from Cape Ball to Rose Spit. The exact locations of the worst conditions change with the shifting sandbars. The "hump" of seas that can develop make some folks afraid to pass around Rose Spit. It is best to keep well into the deeper water when rounding the spit, for strong overfalls occur just off the end, making it particularly dangerous. The conditions are even worse when the southeast winds blow against a flooding tide, which can be as strong as 3.5 knots. The transition, as you round the spit, from shallow to deep water also affects the sea conditions.

When the pressure-slope is east or northeast, the southeast winds hit along the east coast of the Charlottes and pour into Skidegate Inlet, but generally don't hit Queen Charlotte City too hard. All of the headlands will have strong southeast winds. When the pressure-slope turns more to the southeast, a wind shadow will spread up the east coast, and the winds in Skidegate Inlet will be light.

The waves break about 1 to 3 miles off Cape Chroustcheff, just south of Sandspit, and steepen as they cross the bar at the mouth of Skidegate Inlet. The waves also steepen when they encounter tides exiting Cumshewa Inlet. Currents near Cumshewa Head, Skedans Point, Heming Head, and Benjamin Point can be wicked when the tide is changing.

Beware of all headlands and points, for winds and tidal currents may be stronger around them. With the extreme tidal ranges that occur, winds against tides are especially dangerous. It is best to pass the headlands at slack tide, or to give them a wide berth.

167

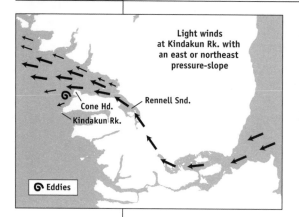

Light winds at Kindakun Rk. with an east or northeast pressure-slope

Cone Hd.

Rennell Snd.

Kindakun Rk.

⟳ Eddies

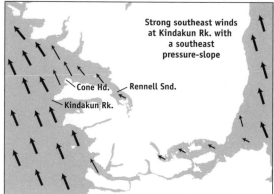

Strong southeast winds at Kindakun Rk. with a southeast pressure-slope

Cone Hd.

Rennell Snd.

Kindakun Rk.

The winds at Kindakun Rock are sensitive to the orientation of the pressure-slope. When the pressure-slope is southeast then the winds at Kindakun will also be southeast, and can rise with a strengthening gradient to gale or storm force. Rennell Sound gets a certain amount of sheltering and lighter winds in this situation. As the pressure-slope backs toward the northeast, however, the winds will pour strongly through Rennell Sound, but Kindakun Rock will get more and more sheltering from Moresby Island, and the winds will switch from the southeast to a light easterly. Winds coming out of Rennell Sound can create eddies, or "spin drifts," around Cone Head. When the pressure-slope is such that easterly winds pass through the inlets on Graham Island, most of the coast north of Tian Head will have light winds.

> As the ocean buoys are low in the water they tend to under report winds. The West Moresby buoy may report 30-35 knots when Kindakun Rock has 40-45 knot winds.

Moresby Island

The narrowness of Moresby Island allows southeast winds along the east side of the island to pass over and hit hard onto the waters of the inlets on the west side. This makes seeking shelter and anchoring a bit of a problem with strong southeast winds. The southernmost part of the Queen Charlotte Islands is particularly difficult in this regard. Gowgaia Bay and Tasu Sound are two examples of places where gusty winds develop after coming down off the mountains.

> When moving into an inlet, observe the trees. If the trees are all leaning over in one direction then watch out for winds from that direction. It is generally OK if the trees are standing up tall, for the winds are likely much less than outside the inlet.

Harriet Harbour, which has a native name meaning place of strong winds, also gets southeast winds that have passed over the mountains and into the harbour. When the pressure-slope is close to southeast, strong southeast winds blow into Rose Harbour, then across the narrow neck of land and the head of the inlet, to give gusty winds in Carpenter Bay. It must also be remembered that places that are safe in southeast winds ahead of the front may not be so safe with the westerly winds that follow the passage of the front.

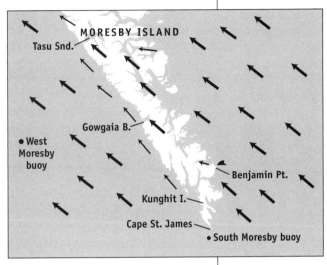

When the winds spill over the mountains they create cat's-paws on the water. They appear, disappear, then move along a short distance before appearing again, as the gusty winds periodically surface.

Downslope winds develop in various inlets when there are strong winds at mountaintop level, perpendicular to the mountain range. A general description of downslope winds is found in Chapter 2. The winds, being trapped between the mountaintop and an inversion above are forced down the lee side of the mountain into the adjacent inlets. Ikeda Cove and Jedway Bay are among the worst for these winds. The winds there can reach 60 knots while the southeast winds outside the inlets are much weaker. The winds surprise mariners for they are perpendicular to the angle of the inlet. Ikeda Cove is an interesting place for it has a high amount of magnetite nearby which affects compass readings.

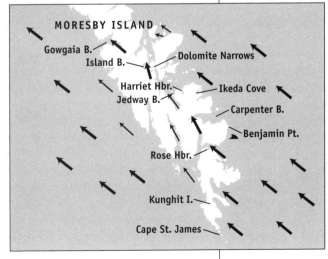

NORTH COAST | QUEEN CHARLOTTE ISLANDS

> One mariner observed a very strong downslope wind in Island Bay just north of Dolomite Narrows (locally called Burnaby Narrows) one September night. The winds came down off the mountains at speeds of 50 to 60 knots. They lasted until the morning, then stopped. There was not a breath of wind outside the narrows when it was windy inside.

When the air is very stable, and the winds aren't too strong, southeast winds blowing into inlets on Moresby Island will bounce off the mountains at the head of the inlet, and come back as westerlies. This can create gusty and confusing winds that can be dangerous.

NORTHERLY PRESSURE-SLOPE WINDS

When the pressure-slope is nearer northeast the outflow that affects the Queen Charlotte Islands comes primarily from Portland Inlet. Normally the outflow from all the inlets eases before it manages to extend all the way to the Charlottes. When there is a strong northeast gradient, however, that extends beyond the Coast Mountains and over the Charlottes, strong winds will pour through all of the mainland inlets and will impact the east side of the Queen Charlotte Islands, and will pass through the gaps that cross the islands. Winds on the west side of the Charlottes will then be varied, being very strong east to northeast near the mouths of the inlets but almost calm away from the inlets.

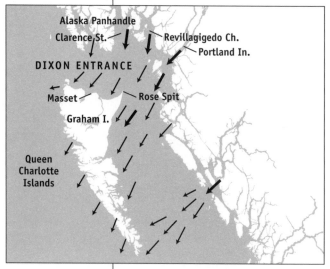

When the pressure-slope is nearer to due north then the outflow winds also come out from the inlets of the Alaska Panhandle. These winds primarily affect just the north coast of Graham Island and eastern Dixon Entrance. In this situation the plume of winds that exits Portland Inlet will move more toward the south and instead of passing out Dixon Entrance will spread down the full length of the Queen Charlotte Islands. The winds again pass through the gaps within the islands and exit out the west side, but this time with a more southerly slant.

The lowest temperature ever recorded on the Charlottes was -25°C at the Canadian Forces base at Masset, on 16 January 1980.

SOUTHERLY PRESSURE-SLOPE WINDS

When southeast winds shift to southwest they ease but become more turbulent. In winter, southwest winds bring poor visibility all along the west coast. The strength of the southwest winds depends largely on the strength of the front, and the rate of pressure rises behind it. Southwest winds in summer aren't as turbulent as in winter but still bring low visibilities.

South to southwest winds and seas that encounter opposing currents around headlands create nasty conditions. Kindakun Point and Hunter Point are two examples of where this occurs, but these conditions are common at all points. The southwest winds also pour through all the inlets across Moresby Island, and funnel out those on the east coast.

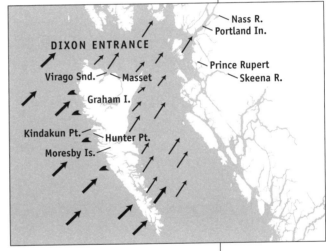

Fog can form in the light southwest to west winds after the passage of a front. A wall of fog can be produced along the north coast of Graham Island. It is usually worst west of Virago Sound, though Masset will also get some, but it is not as dense or as frequent as it is closer to Prince Rupert, and near the Skeena and Nass rivers. Often the fog along the west coast of the Queen Charlotte Islands will lift into low stratus clouds.

WESTERLY PRESSURE-SLOPE WINDS

Northwest winds can hit hard all the way down the west coast of the Charlottes when the pressure-slope is near 220°. They will turn into the inlets during the afternoon. They are funnelled against the higher mountains and produce winds, especially near Cape St. James, that frequently rise to gale force. While winds against the tides can be dangerous all across the coast, the conditions near the complicated tide rips around Cape St. James are extremely dangerous with almost all winds. Tide rips can be a problem all along west Moresby Island, from Gowgaia Bay southward, as northwest winds against the flooding tides produce sizeable breakers.

Diurnal winds

With daytime heating, Moresby Island heats up and creates inflow winds through the inlets, which increase during the afternoon, and drop off in the evening. On some days the winds will howl through the inlets while it will be flat calm outside. But there is something about the inflow winds of Moresby Island that is not experienced along the mainland coast. Moresby Island is narrow and has many inlets on both sides, so the inflow winds that develop through the inlets on one side can pour over the island and pass out through the inlets on the other side. These winds could be compared to the Qualicums and Nimpkish winds of Vancouver Island, but since the southern part of the Queen Charlotte Islands is so much narrower than Vancouver Island, there are more locations where "cross-over-winds" are possible.

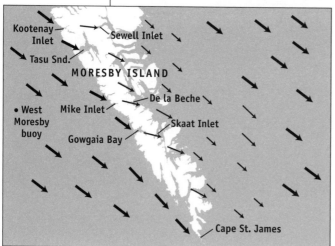

These winds develop through almost all inlets of Moresby Island. Three examples of inlet combinations are: Gowgaia Bay and Skaat Inlet, Kooteney Inlet and Sewell Inlet, and Mike Inlet and De la Beche Inlet. The winds begin to cross the island in the late afternoon, once the strength of winds is such that it can rise up over the adjoining pass.

These winds will only develop when the air is sufficiently unstable, allowing them to go up over the mountains instead of being blocked by them. It also requires an inversion near mountaintop level to cap the flow's upward motion, and deflect it back down to the water level. Without this cap the winds may just whistle above your head and not be felt. A nearby ridge of high pressure, with its subsiding air, could provide the inversion. Downslope winds have similar requirements. The winds may still be strengthened, however, only when the flow comes from just the right direction. Northwest winds, for instance, are

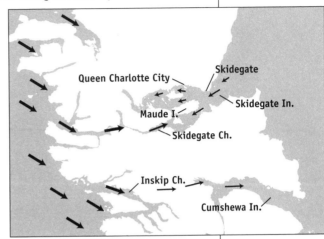

channelled along southern Moresby Island, and create very strong winds off Cape St. James when the direction is just right.

The reverse can also happen, with easterly inflow winds in channels on the east coast passing out into inlets on the west coast. This would not happen at the same pressure-slope orientation that produces northwest winds along the west side of the Charlottes and a west to east cross-over flow, but would occur once the pressure-slope has turned far enough to the northwest that the winds are slack on the west side of the islands. Afternoon inflow winds in Cumshewa (which are southeasterlies), exit through Inskip Channel on the west coast.

> Queen Charlotte City does not frequently get fog, but when it does it burns off around 1000 or 1100 hours, on both sides of the Inlet, with patches lingering in the middle.

Westerly winds that blow into Skidegate Channel get as far as Maude Island where they are met by easterly inflow winds developing along the east side of the Queen Charlotte Islands, in Skidegate Inlet. The easterly inflow winds are strongest on the south side of the channel. During a summer afternoon these two flows can oscillate back and forth, depending on their individual strengths, so that Queen Charlotte City will have westerly winds for a time before they switch to easterly.

Northern mainland coast

The "inside passage" is the main route taken between Port Hardy and Prince Rupert. It follows a variety of channels and passageways that are sheltered most of the time from the winds and waves that affect the open waters of Queen Charlotte Sound and Hecate Strait. But some of these channels, in certain weather patterns, do experience strong winds. This section looks at places and times when these strong winds occur. The north coast, while blessed with an abundance of places to see and explore, has to deal with the fact that its proximity to the Gulf of Alaska, which is the home of many low pressure systems, causes it to have its full share of clouds, rain, and wind. In balance, however, rainbows are a common sight, and nowhere are they more brilliant than here.

EASTERLY PRESSURE-SLOPE WINDS

The radar wind images in the previous chapter show the full range of possible easterly winds across the north coast. They affect the Queen Charlotte Islands most when the pressure-slope is more toward the northeast, and affect the mainland coast when the pressure-slope is closer to the southeast. The mainland inlets generally have light northeast winds throughout the entire range of easterly pressure-slope winds.

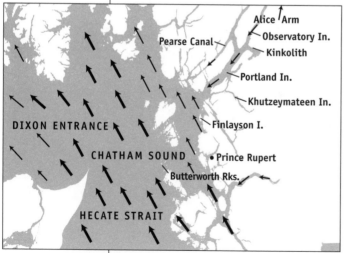

Chatham Sound

Chatham Sound lies on the dividing line between the southeast winds of Hecate Strait, and the northeast winds of the coastal inlets. The radar picture for 12 January 2002 shows the last remnants of northeast winds in the far north, as southeast winds strengthen and push up into the sound. The mouth of Portland Inlet is potentially dangerous when northeast winds persist in the canal, while southeast winds are strengthening in Chatham Sound. When tides are added to this mix the seas can build to 4 or 5 metres, and with crests only three metres apart. Butterworth Rocks is bad when tides and southeast winds meet.

Prince Rupert, a gateway to the north coast, is a city of 17,000. It is surrounded by the most beautiful wilderness areas of the world, which include fjords, rain forests, lagoons, sandy beaches, and haunting abandoned villages. Cow Bay is one of the oldest parts of Prince Rupert. It is now a "funky" shopping and dining area. It originally got its name when a Swiss farmer, who barged in a herd of cattle, did not have a place to land them so he put them into the bay to swim ashore.

Southeast winds build steep waves near Finlayson Island, and produce gusty conditions inside Prince Rupert Harbour. In most situations, even when the winds are nearly southerly as the front passes, the winds do not blow with any strength up Pearse Canal.

Alice Arm was named after Alice, wife of the Rev. Robert Tomlinson. Immediately after their wedding day in Victoria in 1868, Alice and her new husband journeyed for 24 days in a large Haida canoe to their mission station at Kincolith. Observatory Inlet was named by Captain Vancouver in 1793, since he set up an observatory there to check the rate of his chronometers and correct his fixing of latitude and longitude.

Edye Passage, at the top end of Porcher Island, is a place to cross with caution. Southeast winds move from Kitkatla Inlet over the peninsula into Welcome Harbour, then into the passage to meet the winds that come down off the mountains of Porcher Island. Bands of very strong winds are created. These downslope winds also affect the waters of Refuge Bay. It has been noted that if Holland Rock, just 10 miles northeast of Edye Passage, is getting 20 knot winds, then it could be 30 to 35 knots in Edye Passage. Similarly if 40 knots are being reported in Hecate Strait, then the winds in Edye Passage could be gusting as high as 80 knots.

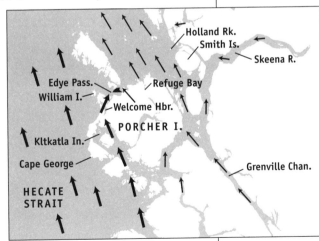

Winds are stronger over the deeper waters west of Porcher Island than they are close to the island. When heading out into Hecate Strait you will begin to feel the swell near William Island, and get the full force of the wind once outside

NORTHERN MAINLAND COAST

Cape George. Southeast winds passing around the back side of Porcher Island create steep standing waves as they meet the outflow from the Skeena River, just off Smith Island. This area at the mouth of the Skeena River also has standing waves during a flooding tide.

Grenville Channel area

When strong southeast winds hit the mainland coast sizeable seas develop all along the eastern side of Hecate Strait from Aristazabal Island to Banks Island. Steep waves build against the ebb tides coming out of Otter and Langley Passages.

The winds in Grenville Channel are highly dependent on the exact direction of the pressure-slope. If the pressure-slope is northeast there will be no winds in Grenville, but when it veers toward the southeast the southeast winds funnel through the channel, producing winds that are potentially higher than in Hecate Strait. Klewnuggit Inlet is so aligned that it gets all of the southeast winds that are in Grenville Channel.

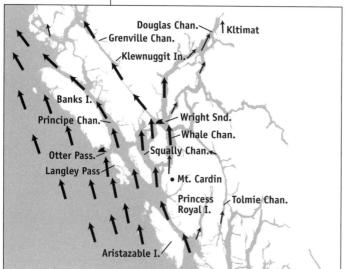

The seas that develop in Grenville Channel are not normally as high as in Hecate Strait. The development of seas is limited by the maximum 50 mile fetch, which is the approximate length of the channel. At the western end of the channel the seas can build to 2.6 metres with a 30 knot wind, and to 4.8 metres with 50 knots. Principe Channel can get the same strength of winds as in Hecate Strait when the pressure-slope is from the southeast, but like Grenville Channel, only wind waves are created, and no swell waves are present. When the pressure-slope is from the east or northeast, both Grenville and Principe Channels will have lighter winds than Hecate, and as a result, mariners take refuge here.

Bill Hickman, a long-time pilot and manager of RivTow in Kitimat said, "Only one in five weather systems that bring strong southeasterly winds to Hecate Strait will produce strong southerly winds in Douglas Channel." To the author's knowledge, no study has been done on the proportion of storms that affect the coastal inlets compared to the outer waters, but this ratio of one to five seems about right.

Wright Sound, Whale Channel, and Squally Channel can all be wild with southeast winds. Wright Sound is particularly bad, for it has five channels leading into it, so no matter what the pressure-slope direction there is a good chance that one of the channels will be experiencing strong winds. When northerly winds continue to flow out of Douglas Channel into Wright Sound, and southeasterlies come up from the south, the seas steepen and become chaotic. The western part of Wright Sound gets some protection from northerlies coming out of Douglas Channel. Gusty southeast downslope winds come down off Mt. Cardin on Princess Royal Island, and cross the harbour into Whale Channel. Both Tolmie Channel and Princess Royal Channel get southeast winds but they are not as strong as in Douglas Channel.

Milbanke Sound

Milbanke Sound gets hit hard with both southeast and southwest winds. Oscar and Moss passages are generally okay with true southeast winds, but when the winds turn more southerly they will turn into the passages and will be particularly bad, especially when against the tide. During most autumn and winter seasons it is normal to get five or six storms with 40 to 50 knot winds, with some of them reaching 60 to 80 knots. Southeast winds also funnel up

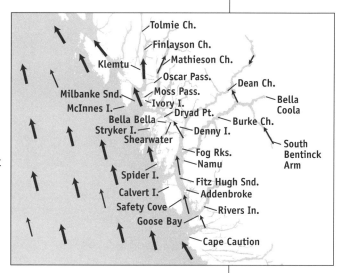

Finlayson Channel fairly regularly, and are stronger than in Tolmie Channel. Mathieson Channel also gets strong southeast winds during the nastier storms when the pressure-slope is close to southeast. The Shearwater area generally gets stronger southeast winds than at Bella Bella. Storm force winds come down off Denny Island and move onto the waters off Shearwater.

177

McInnes I. and Ivory I. represent fairly well the winds in Milbanke Sound and the area off Shearwater and Bella Bella, but Dryad Point represents little more than itself.

One of the worst storms experienced at Shearwater occurred late on 24 November 2000. A Department of Fisheries and Oceans boat tied up at the dock measured a wind of 78 knots. Likely this was a peak gust, for McInnes Island and Egg Island both reported 55 knots with higher gusts. Dryad, Ivory, and Addenbroke all reported 30 to 34 knots with higher gusts. Cathedral Point remained light northeast until the early morning of the next day. The pressure-slope during the time of the peak winds changed from 120° to 160°.

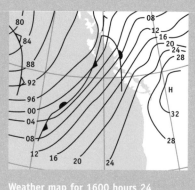

Weather map for 1600 hours 24 November 2000.

While winds in Dean and Burke channels remain light with southeast winds offshore, southeast winds do affect South Bentinck Arm. Southeast winds that blow up Fitz Hugh Sound are worse at the northern end, near Namu, than in the south off Addenbroke. Namu, the place of many winds, can occasionally get strong easterly winds that come down off the lake behind Namu with speeds up to 90 knots, creating downbursts and waterspouts, which form in the appropriately named Whirlwind Bay. The light station at Addenbroke is sheltered from most southeast winds by the hills to the south.

Addenbroke was originally called Addenbrooke when it was established in 1914 but was changed by some early cartographer and never changed back. A lightkeeper once rowed the 80 miles from Addenbroke to Bella Bella and back in 2½ days to get help for a newborn baby.

Southeast winds, and the southerly swell, tend to be stronger on the west side of Fitz Hugh Sound, while the tidal currents are stronger on the east side. The tidal currents are particularly sloppy near Fog Rocks. Safety Cove on Calvert Island, as the name suggests, is a good place to hide from southeast winds. Spider and Stryker Island, on the edge of Hecate Strait, get strong southeast winds, while there may be very little at Shearwater. Goose Bay, at the mouth of Rivers Inlet, is bad with southeast winds, as air cascades down the mountains to produce strong gusty winds, but since the wind is coming off the land the waters are calm.

Coastal inlets

The winds through the inlets remain from the northeast throughout the range of pressure-slopes that create easterly winds over open waters, and only turn into the south once the pressure-slope veers beyond 130°. In most cases, as a front passes and the pressure-slope veers toward the southeast, the winds ease. Thus by the time the pressure-slope has tilted far enough around to propel strong winds up the inlets there is little strength remaining in the pressure gradient, and hence no winds of any note. Strong winds do occasionally move up the inlets but this is discussed later in the section on southerly pressure-slopes.

NORTHERLY PRESSURE-SLOPE WINDS

The coastal inlets are the main artery for northerly winds to pass from the BC interior onto the coast. The other channels are affected in various degrees depending on their orientation. Portland Inlet, Douglas Channel, and Dean and Burke channels have all had winds well up in the storm force wind category, and several of them have touched hurricane force strengths. The Skeena Valley also experiences strong outflow winds. Pearse Canal, just next to Portland Inlet, generally gets less winds and noticeably lower seas. Steamer Passage provides some protection from the outflow winds. In the classic arctic outflow events the temperature drops enough so that freezing spray becomes a significant problem. Cold air at the head of the inlets can create sea ice, especially where fresh water enters the inlet.

Pearse Canal
Portland In.
Steamer Pass.
Grey I.
Dundas I.
Green I.
Skeena R.
Holland Rk.

Grey Islet and Green Island are good indicators of outflow from Portland Inlet. Holland Rock represents the outflow from the Skeena River. The Douglas Channel buoy reports outflow winds but they are generally 20 or 30% less than in other parts of the inlet. Cathedral Point is a good representation of the winds in Dean and Burke channels.

Green Island in a freezing spray event.

Grenville and Douglas Channel

The outflow from Douglas Channel spreads everywhere in Whale Channel, and to a lesser extent in Squally Channel. The small channels that run at right angles

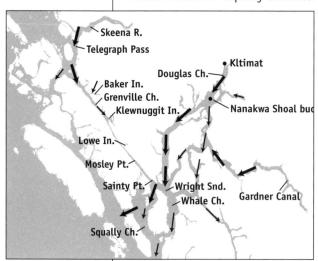

between the main outflow inlets generally have light winds. Several mariners said that Grenville Channel will blow with a northerly outflow, even though the channel is perpendicular to the direction of Douglas Channel. Perhaps, if the pressure-slope is far enough to the north the flow from the Skeena River will turn down Telegraph Passage and affect the top of Grenville Channel. The very bottom of Grenville Channel could be affected by winds coming out of Douglas Channel. Northeasterly winds that blow over the tops of the Coast Mountains will occasionally descend down off the mountains on the north side of Grenville Channel, and hit the waters between Mosley Point and Sainty Point. Similar downslope winds of 30 knots have also been reported in Baker Inlet.

> The tides enter Grenville Channel from both ends and meet near Klewnuggit Inlet, where the tidal conditions can be very chaotic. While the separation of the ebb tide takes place about one mile to the northwest, the exact meeting and separation points change with the winds outside. Eddies develop with the ebbing stream off Lowe Inlet.

The wave conditions through the inlets are limited by the available fetch. Some of the longest possible fetch lengths (without a 30 degree change in direction) are only about 30 miles, which means that a 40 knot wind can create, at most, a three metre sea, and a 65 knot wind, a four metre sea. Since the fetch is limited in the shorter secondary inlets the seas are choppy, but not extreme. In Douglas Channel the strong outflow winds bounce off the steep sides of the channel causing the worst wave conditions to be near the edges of the channel because of reflecting winds and waves from the sides of the channel meeting the main flow of the channel.

Douglas Channel to Milbanke Sound

Graham Reach of Princess Royal Channel and Tolmie Channel get strong northerly winds after they have passed down Devastation Channel and across the peninsula into Ursula Channel. These northerly winds weaken by the time they reach Klemtu. If there are 30 or 40 knot winds in Tolmie Channel, Klemtu will get only 10 to 15 knots.

> Kitimat, which comes from the Haisla word for "people of the snow," had a near-record snowfall of 140cm (4 feet, 7 inches) within a 24 hour period on 11 February 1999.

Gardner Canal gets strong outflow winds, which some say can be 10 to 15 knots stronger that in Burke Channel. The path of the outflow into Gardner Canal is from the interior and along the Kemano River. Winds as high as 100 knots have been recorded in the canal. The winds are northerly when they enter the canal but turn into easterlies as they pass down toward Staniforth Point, at the south end of Devastation Channel. Corkscrew eddies, which push the water downward, are created as the winds round the dog-leg turn in the canal.

As the depth of arctic air increases following several days of cold outflow conditions, outflow winds will develop in various other channels, such as Spiller and Mathieson. The outflow in Mathieson Channel is connected to the outflow from Gardner Canal, via a pass between Chief Mathews Bay and Mussel Inlet. The winds through Mathieson are still very strong as they pass the eastern end of Oscar Passage but begin to ease as they pass Ivory

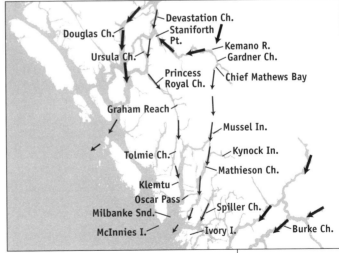

Island, and are even weaker by the time they reach McInnes Island. Strong eddies, or willi-waws, form off the steep sides of the Kynoch Inlet.

> Bella Bella (Waglisla), home of the Heiltsuk Native Band, is now the largest community on the central coast with a population of approximately 1200 people.

NORTH COAST | **NORTHERN MAINLAND COAST**

Northeast winds coming down Dean Channel pass over northern Denny Island, into Shearwater Harbour, into McLoughlin Bay, and then down into the western entrance of Lama Pass. Bella Bella lies just to the north of the main plume of winds, and misses the worst of it. The conditions at the bottom of King Island can be very nasty where the flow from Dean and Fisher channels meets the outflow from Burke. Except in these extreme cold outflow situations the winds generally ease soon after leaving Fitz Hugh Sound. Icing conditions can be severe in all of these channels and can be nasty as far down as Hakai Pass. An elder remembered a time around 1953 when two centimetres of ice developed on the waters off Bella Bella. Cousins Inlet freezes over from just off Ocean Falls to Wearing Point.

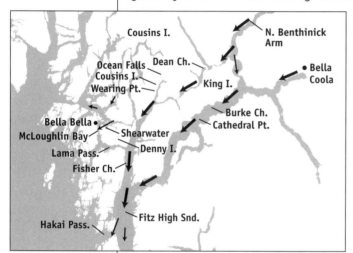

Outflow winds are the only ones that are a problem in Bella Coola. It can get storm force winds which pass from the interior across the Bella Coola River. Dean and Burke channels both have easy access through passes to the interior so winds there blow very strongly in outflow conditions. A number of mariners suggested that the outflow through Burke is stronger than in Dean, but others suggested that they are about the same, except that Dean can be more difficult because of stronger tidal currents. Crossing Burke Channel in a strong outflow is extremely difficult, if not impossible.

> Local knowledge says that northeast winds at Cathedral Point need to rise above 30 knots before they get any wind at Shearwater. But when Cathedral is 40 knots, Shearwater will be 10 knots, and then after that they both rise together. In most winters the Shearwater area gets two or three weeks of outflow. Another mariner similarly said that if Bella Coola has a 70 knot outflow, then Bella Bella will get about 25 to 30 knots.

It is important to remember that as the pressure gradient changes, the winds change from being strong in one inlet to being strong in another. The following example given by George Newson illustrates this. One day, George was travelling

through Hakai Passage, getting severe icing from cold outflow winds, but once he turned into Fitz Hugh Sound it went flat calm. The winds remained light until he got near Egg Island where he started to get a strong outflow from Rivers Inlet. The explanation of this is connected to the fact that when the pressure-slope is more easterly the outflow winds coming down Fisher Channel join that from Burke Channel, and flow into Hakai Pass instead of going farther down Fitz Hugh Sound. The next place that would get the more easterly winds is near the mouth of Rivers Inlet. When the pressure-slope is more northerly, the outflow winds pass all the way down Fitz Hugh Sound, and do not turn into Hakai Pass.

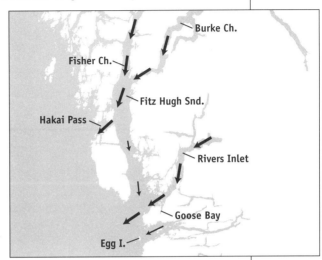

Rivers Inlet only gets a strong outflow after the high over the interior is well established and the winds have been blowing for two or three days. It gets gale force winds when there are storm force winds in Burke Channel. In Goose Bay, at the mouth of Rivers Inlet, the outflow wind comes around the corner and goes down in a swirling descending motion that depresses the water.

SOUTHERLY PRESSURE-SLOPE WINDS

Coastal inlets primarily blow either northerly outflow or southerly inflow at any time during the year. The southerly inflow arises either from the strong southerly winds that develop behind a front, with a southerly pressure-slope, or with summertime heating of the walls of the inlets. "Southwest winds are readily made, and quickly even," said Gary Housty, a long-time fisherman in Bella Bella. Doug Sharkey from Shearwater also described southwest winds as not being a big concern for they are "usually very short and rare - a passing disaster." Southwest winds come up fast, they can be dangerous and scary, but generally die away quickly. They are most common in the transition periods of spring and early autumn. The summer inflow is discussed in the section on westerly pressure-slope winds, for they are primarily caused by daytime heating.

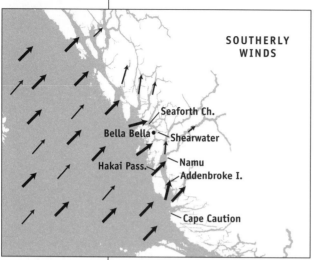

SOUTHERLY WINDS

Seaforth Ch.

Bella Bella • Shearwater

Hakai Pass. Namu
Addenbroke I.

Cape Caution

Southwest winds can be bad in places such as east of Dundas Island where they are funnelled, and have a long fetch building fairly high seas. Inlets that are open to the southwest, such as Seaforth Channel and Hakai Passage can be rough as southwest wind waves and swell are able to pour directly into them and may increase in height through funnelling. Namu Harbour and Addenbroke both receive southwest winds that pass through these inlets. The waters off Cape Caution receive the full thrust of southwest winds.

WESTERLY PRESSURE-SLOPE WINDS

Westerly winds across the coast are affected primarily by the strength and orientation of the ridge of high pressure that typically lies off the coast during the summer. These winds that are created through pressure differences were given the name "offshore-ridge" winds. During the summer the strong heating from the sun modifies the winds so that they have a daily, or diurnal, cycle of strengthening and weakening. These winds are called "diurnal winds." The overall pattern is set by the strength and orientation of the ridge, which affects the pressure-slope, but is modified by heating effects over the land. The pressure-slope winds most affect the open waters and the areas adjacent to them, while the diurnal effects are strongest farther inland, especially near the inlets. The same inlets that have strong northerly outflow winds in winter have strong southerly inflow winds in summer, for the strength of both outflow and inflow are connected to the temperatures over the interior plateau. If the interior heats up strongly during the afternoon then the cool coastal air is sucked up into the inlets. The warmer the interior, the stronger the inflow. This is exactly the reverse of winter outflow, which is dependent on significant cooling over the interior. Inflow will happen every day in the summer, unless there is a weak low and cloudy skies over the coast.

Offshore-ridge westerly winds

Northwest winds that spread through Dixon Entrance do not immediately hit ashore along Chatham Sound. They need to first overcome the nightly outflow winds. But once the northwest winds do reach the coast they tend to wrap around all the islands and are difficult to escape from, and as a result have been called the worst winds in Chatham Sound. They can create a heavy buildup of seas at the mouth of Portland Inlet, and at the entrance to Prince Rupert Harbour. The worst situation is when a 30 knot wind is blowing up into Portland Inlet, and there is a seven metre ebbing tide coming out. The combination can produce three to four metre seas, about three metres apart, the impact of which is not to be underestimated.

Offshore-ridge
WESTERLY
WINDS

Chatham Snd. Portland In.
Dundas I. Khutzeymateen In.
Dixon Entrance Work Ch.
Triple I. Lucy I.
Prince Rupert
Skeena R.
Grenville Ch. Douglas Ch.
Hecate Strait Principe Ch.
Banks I.
Estevan Snd.

> When kayaking near Prince Rupert listen to Triple Island and Lucy Island. If Lucy is over 10 knots, then consider seriously before doing a long crossing.

As the pressure-slope turns from the southwest to west the winds blow down the length of Hecate Strait. The first places affected are the outer mainland coast islands. Laredo Channel and Milbanke Sound, for instance, are affected by northwest winds, but many channels farther inside are not, and remain with light winds except for those caused by local heating. Northwest winds spread into Principe Channel, Grenville Channel, and Estevan Sound, and may even be stronger than outside due to funnelling. Locations directly downwind of islands have much lighter winds.

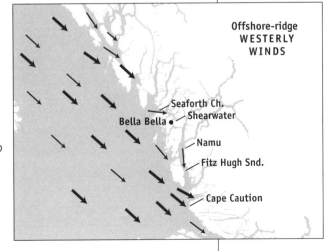

Offshore-ridge
WESTERLY
WINDS

Seaforth Ch.
Shearwater
Bella Bella
Namu
Fitz Hugh Snd.
Cape Caution

185

| **NORTHERN MAINLAND COAST**

The Bella Bella and Shearwater area are examples of locations that are not strongly affected by northwest winds. Bays on the east side of islands such as Calvert Island are safe for anchorage with westerly winds, while places such as Namu that open to the west are not. The upper winds may be strong north-westerlies, as seen in the movement of clouds, but the winds remain aloft and do not come down to the surface. Each channel steers the winds according to its own orientation, hence the winds may be westerly in Seaforth Channel, but almost northerly in Fitz Hugh Sound.

Diurnal winds

Along the northern mainland coast the diurnal winds are some form of westerly and, since the sea breeze wind direction more or less coincides with the

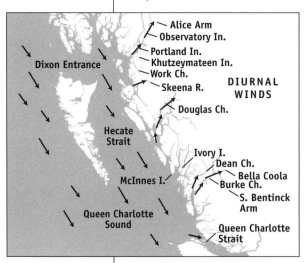

prevailing westerlies, they are enhanced. On the east side of the Queen Charlotte Islands, however, the sea breeze wind is easterly, which may weaken, or totally overcome the prevailing westerly winds, depending on their relative strengths. The inlets generally have northerly outflow winds in the morning that persist until heating starts to draw the winds up the inlets. With strong diurnal heating the northwest winds over Hecate Strait are drawn closer to the mainland coast and add to the afternoon inflow through the inside channels.

Dan Wakeman, who gives tours in the Khutzeymateen Grizzly Bear Sanctuary, normally leaves Alice Arm, at the head of Observatory Inlet, at first light so that he will have 6 to 8 hours to get out of the inlet before the winds get too strong. Travel in Portland Inlet should be done before noon, as the winds in the afternoon and evening can be dangerous.

The winds normally begin near 1000 hours, and gradually increase in strength until late afternoon, then ease fairly quickly around 1800 or 1900 hours. All of the mainland inlets experience inflow winds that typically peak near 20 to 25 knots in the afternoon. In the extreme event, at the head of the inlets, these winds may rise to gale force. The larger channels such as Portland Inlet, Skeena River, Douglas, Dean, and Burke channels all have connections to the interior and have stronger inflow winds than the smaller inlets. These winds, as with northerly outflow, take on the direction of the channel. The afternoon inflow gradually increases up the inlet, and is strongest near the head. In Burke Channel, for example, the winds are continually funnelled up the inlet and are worst near the community of Bella Coola. Inflow winds also develop in South Bentinck Arm.

These channels also all have straight stretches where the fetch is large enough to build significant seas. Inflow winds through Work Channel increase during the afternoon but are rarely dangerous. It has been said that if you get one metre of sea in Work Channel there will be two metres in Portland Inlet.

Clouds that limit daytime heating can change all the patterns described above. Without heating from the sun, the winds don't develop. Fog that commonly extends from southern Hecate Strait along the central coast and into Queen Charlotte Strait, slows the heating over the areas close to the open water, but increases the contrast of temperature between the coast and the inlets farther inland. Fog goes through a diurnal cycle that was previously described in the region, "Chatham Point to Port Hardy."

> **McInnes Island and Ivory Island light stations are both good indicators of northwest winds.**

Drainage outflow winds are also part of the diurnal wind. While southerly inflow winds develop during the late morning and afternoon, the northerly outflow winds develop overnight. The strength of the outflow depends on the strength of the westerly pressure-slope gradient and the amount of snow that remains on the mountaintops. When the gradient is strong the southerly inflow winds last longer. They weaken through the evening and night but since they do not completely disappear until quite late, there is little time for the northerly winds to strengthen. When the mountains are still covered with snow, as they are in the spring and early summer, there is a continual push of cold winds down into the inlets, which is only overcome by a strong inflow gradient. The northerly part of the cycle is then stronger, and remains so, until the snow melts. The higher coastal mountains that maintain snow year-round continue to create drainage winds throughout the summer, but they tend to only affect the upper reaches of the larger inlets.

T. Reimchen discovered that salmon provide significant amounts of nitrogen for the growth of the coastal forest. Bears spread salmon carcasses quite some distance away from coastal streams.

FINAL COMMENTS

The cycle of the year and the global picture are part of the big picture of weather.

Weather is more than wind and waves, clouds and rain. It is part of a moving, ever-changing flow that encompasses the entire earth and is shared by all. Living with weather is what we do here on earth. Knowledge and understanding of weather is a crucial element for those of us who live, work, and play on the waters of the BC coast.

While preparing this book several people told me to "keep it simple" and this request has haunted me. The weather is too complex for me to provide an in-depth description in a simple fashion and much more could have been said if space and focus had allowed. But in spite of this, I trust that this book will help lift the veil of apparent chaos that prevents us from seeing patterns and rhythms in the weather that swirls around us. The cycle of the year and the global picture are part of the big picture of weather. The weather experienced at any moment is the smallest, most personal aspect. Allow your vision to encompass the variety of weather that spans these two perspectives.

In 2002 the weather has varied in a number of ways from what we might consider normal. Some of these variations have been attributed to El Niño or global warming. But whatever their cause they show that weather patterns are complex and are affected by many forces, some of which we may not understand or even recognize.

The journey is ended. The path taken by this book moved from an imaginative picture of weather, to the impact that the BC coast has on the moving fluids of air and water, to a consideration of the many weather patterns and the sorting of them into five basic patterns, and then finally to the comments about local conditions. These comments came primarily from mariners who live and work on the BC coast, and are a mere sampling of the many localized variations of winds and waves that occur. If more mariners were spoken to, or spoken to in greater depth with more revealing questions, then many other interesting and important comments would have been gathered and shared in this book. But now that this book is finished it is up to you, the reader, to take this path of understanding further, by adding your own experiences to what has been discussed here.

appendix

SUMMARIZING THE TOPICS

appendix

Weather, as it has been described in this book, can vary dramatically across the BC coast. The first step of interpreting the present and future weather is making your own observation. What does the sky look like where you are? What are your winds? What are the conditions on the water, including the waves from the local winds, waves from distant storms, and how are they both modified by local tidal currents? These are questions that are normally answered by a quick look outside. Some mariners have found that it is very useful to keep a weather log. Keeping a log not only allows you to keep track of the dates of notable weather events, and possibly more importantly to note what conditions preceded them, but it can also be a significant part in the process of learning more about your own local weather patterns.

> Watch the sky. An intense steel grey foreboding look indicates that a weather system is close. Remember, even if reasonably calm, the winds can rise quickly. One can travel in a diminishing gale, but building winds are more dangerous.

Once you have taken your own observation, the next step is to check on observations from various sites around you. Local knowledge will soon tell you that certain observations are good indicators of conditions in various waters while other observation sites are not as useful. Certain observation sites will be more important in one weather pattern but less important in others. Observation sites closer to the weather system that is moving your way may give indications of changes to come.

The next step is to listen to the weather forecast. A look at the latest weather map or satellite picture can also help with your understanding of how conditions will develop over the coming hours and days.

MARINE WEATHER FORECASTS

The marine forecast is issued 4 times a day at 0400, 1030, 1600, and 2130 hours local time. Amendments or warnings are issued as required. The forecast is valid for 24 hours with an outlook for the following 24 hours. The synopsis gives an overall picture of the weather systems that are expected to affect the coast, and a summary of the winds. The forecast winds are for the main

The first step of interpreting the present and future weather is making your own observation.

waterways and may not reflect the winds through the islands and passageways at the coastal edge. The forecast seas for the northern and outer waters are the significant wave heights, which are the combined total of wind waves and swell. The cloud and precipitation that are expected are also mentioned.

The wind speed terms, and their definitions, that are used in the synopsis and outlook are as follows:

light	1-10 knots
moderate	11-19 knots
strong	20-33 knots
gale	34-47 knots
storm	48-63 knots
hurricane force	64 knots or more

Wind warnings are only flagged in the forecast when winds of warning strength are expected to occur during the 24 hour period of the forecast. Winds of warning categories may be mentioned in the outlook without a warning being issued or flagged in the text of the forecast. Small craft warnings are based solely on the wind speed range of 20 to 33 knots and are not dependent upon the size of the vessel. Small craft warnings are issued as required, for the inner south coast waters, from Good Friday to November 11.

WEATHER MAPS

Weather maps can be received on H.F. radio facsimile broadcasts or through the internet (the Meteorological Service of Canada web site is found at: "weatheroffice.ec.gc.ca"). The maps can be for various levels of the atmosphere, but the one most likely wanted by the mariner is the surface chart. There are analysis and forecast surface weather maps. The analysis maps are based on observations taken at specific UTC hours. UTC stands for Universal Coordinated Time, and is sometimes referred to as GMT, for Greenwich Mean Time. In some instances these times are labelled with a "Z" based on a division of the globe into 24 zones, each with a letter identifier. UTC is 8 hours ahead of PST, 7 hours ahead of PDT. The normal analysis times are 0000, 0600, 1200, and 1800 UTC, which translate to 1600, 2200, 0400, and 1000 PST. The forecast maps are based on one of these four times and are valid for various periods into the future. Typically the forecast maps are valid for 12, 24, 36, and 48 hours after the initial time, but can extend out to 120 hours (5 days), or even longer.

The analysis maps have lines that join points with the same pressure. These lines are called isobars. North American maps draw isobars every four millibars (a unit of pressure), while in Europe they are often drawn every five millibars. The isobars show areas of higher and lower pressure.

First find on the map your own location, then see where the main weather systems - the highs, lows, and fronts - are located with respect to your location. The winds and weather associated with various weather patterns have been discussed in the earlier chapters. Use the pressure-slope concept, and possibly the compass found at the beginning of Chapter 3, on each map, both analysis and forecast, to categorize the weather into specific patterns. Note the movements of the various features through the period covered by the forecast maps and expect changes in both winds and weather accordingly.

SATELLITE PICTURES

Satellite pictures are available through various sources. They are seen on TV and can be accessed on H.F. radio facsimile broadcasts and on the internet. The picture itself can be one of three types, visual, infrared, and water vapour. The visual picture normally shows much more detail, but is only available during daylight hours. The infrared picture, which basically senses temperatures, is shown with specific colours assigned to certain temperature ranges. It is avail-able both day and night. During the daylight hours it is also possible to see satellite pictures that have both visual and infrared images overlapped. This overlapping can provide a visual sense for higher and lower clouds. The pictures available from the Meteorological Service of Canada at "weatheroffice.ec.gc.ca" show the higher cloud in bluish shades with the lower cloud in yellow tones. Where the clouds are particularly thick they show up as white. Satellite pictures are usually available in both single pictures and in animated loops of several pictures. The water vapour pictures are taken using a different part of the energy spectrum and represent the total water content of the mid-levels of the atmosphere. When seen in animation the water vapour pictures clearly show the fluid-like nature of the atmosphere.

A complete description of satellite pictures would require a book unto itself, so only a brief overview can be given here.

Fronts often lie near the back edge of the cloud that spirals into a low. The clouds on the outer or leading edge of the frontal cloud band will be cirrus. The clouds thicken into cirrostratus, altostratus and nimbostratus closer to the front. The cloud cells found in the colder air behind the front are cumulus or cumulonimbus clouds. Stratocumulus clouds may form under the higher frontal clouds, or may arise from an amalgamation of the cumulus clouds behind the front. Low stratus and fog will show as flat, almost featureless clouds that appear between weather systems. The edge of stratus clouds is often connected to the topography of the coastline. It may appear unmoving as higher clouds move by, but may also change with diurnal heating.

27 May 2002
Ci - cirrus
CS - cirrostratus
AS - Altostratus
NS - Nimbostratus
CB -cumulonimbus
Cu - cumulus

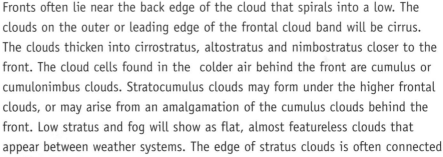

Clear areas result from downward moving air under regions of high pressure, in the dryer air just behind a front, and in downslope, or subsiding winds on the lee side of mountain ranges. These subsidence breaks can often be seen with southwesterly winds blowing across the mountains of the coast, and downwind of many interior mountain ranges.

WIND SPEED FROM WEATHER MAPS

Method of wind speed estimation

The diagram below provides a method to determine the normal peak wind from a weather map. The average wind would be about 70% of the peak wind value. The method works best over open ocean waters but will still give a rough guide for winds within coastal areas.

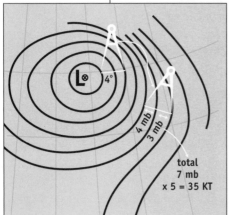

To use this method, first measure on the weather map a distance of 4° of longitude at the latitude of interest. Determine the pressure difference across this measurement. Multiply this pressure difference by 5 to get the approximate peak wind speed. This works well for latitudes between 40°N and 60°N. If, for example, the pressure difference over 4° is 7 mb, then the estimated peak wind would be 35 knots. The mean wind would be near 25 knots. The same calculation can also be done by measuring the pressure difference over 2° of longitude and multiplying the result by 10.

WAVE HEIGHTS

Waves are created by winds blowing over the water. They are controlled by three factors: wind speed, fetch, and duration. Swell waves are not generated by local winds but come from distant storms. Swell waves lengthen and take on a more rounded profile over time. The significant wave height values used in the marine forecast are the combination of local wind waves and swell.

Significant wave height graphs (metres)

Duration 3 hours Wind (knots)	Fetch (nautical miles) 10	20	30	40	50	60	80	120
10	0.4	0.4	0.4	0.4	0.4	0.4	0.4	0.4
20	0.9	1.0	1.0	1.0	1.0	1.0	1.0	1.0
30	1.4	1.8	1.8	1.8	1.8	1.8	1.8	1.8
40	2.0	2.6	2.7	2.7	2.7	2.7	2.7	2.7
50	2.5	3.3	3.7	3.7	3.7	3.7	3.8	3.8
60	3.1	4.1	4.9	4.9	4.9	4.9	5.0	5.0
70	3.7	5.0	5.9	6.2	6.2	6.2	6.2	6.2
80	4.3	5.8	6.9	7.5	7.5	7.5	7.5	7.5

Duration 6 hours Wind (knots)	Fetch (nautical miles) 10	20	30	40	50	60	80	120
10	0.4	0.5	0.5	0.5	0.5	0.5	0.5	0.5
20	0.9	1.1	1.3	1.4	1.4	1.4	1.4	1.4
30	1.4	1.8	2.1	2.4	2.5	2.5	2.6	2.6
40	1.9	2.6	3.0	3.4	3.7	4.0	4.0	4.0
50	2.5	3.3	4.0	4.4	4.8	5.2	5.5	5.5
60	3.1	4.1	4.9	5.5	6.0	6.5	7.2	7.2
70	3.7	5.0	5.9	6.6	7.2	7.8	8.8	9.0
80	4.3	5.8	6.9	7.7	8.5	9.1	10.3	10.9

Duration 12 hours Wind (knots)	Fetch (nautical miles) 10	20	30	40	50	60	80	120
10	0.4	0.5	0.5	0.6	0.6	0.6	0.6	0.6
20	0.9	1.1	1.3	1.4	1.6	1.7	1.8	1.9
30	1.4	1.8	2.1	2.4	2.6	2.8	3.1	3.6
40	1.9	2.6	3.0	3.4	3.7	4.0	4.5	5.2
50	2.5	3.3	4.0	4.4	4.8	5.2	5.6	6.9
60	3.1	4.1	4.4	5.5	6.0	6.5	7.3	8.6
70	3.7	5.0	5.9	6.6	7.2	7.8	8.8	10.3
80	4.3	5.8	6.9	7.7	8.5	9.1	10.3	12.1

BEAUFORT WIND SCALE

Beaufort force	Mariner's description	Wind speed and wave height		Effect of wind at sea
		knots	metres (feet)	
0	calm	0-1		sea like a mirror
1	light air	1-3	0.1 (.3)	ripples with the appearance of scales form, but without foam crests
2	light breeze	4-6	.2-.3 (.5-1)	small wavelets; short but more pronounced; crests do not break
3	gentle breeze	7-10	.6-1.0 (2-3)	larger wavelets; crests begin to break, foam of glassy appearance; perhaps some scattered white horses
4	moderate breeze	11-16	.7-1.5 (2-4.5)	small waves becoming longer; fairly frequent white horses
5	fresh breeze	17-21	1.5-2 (4.5-7)	moderate waves taking a more pronounced long form; many white horses; chance of some spray
6	strong breeze	22-27	2-3.5 (7-11)	long waves begin to form; white foam crests are more extensive; spray likely
7	near gale	28-33	3-4.5 (10-15)	sea heaps up; white foam from breaking waves begins to be blown in streaks along the direction of the wind
8	fresh gale	34-40	4.5-6 (15-20)	moderately high waves of greater length; edges of crests begin to break into the spindrift; the foam is blown in well-marked streaks downwind
9	strong gale	41-47	5.5-7.5 (17-25)	high waves; dense streaks of foam downwind; crests of waves begin to roll over; spray may affect visibility
10	storm	48-55	7-10 (23-33)	very high waves with long overhanging crests; foam in great patches blown in dense white streaks downwind; surface of the sea takes a white appearance, the tumbling of the sea becomes heavy and shock-like; visibility affected
11	violent storm	56-63	9-12.5 (28-42)	exceptionally high waves (small and medium-sized ships lost to view for a time); sea covered with long white patches of foam blown downwind, everywhere wave crests blown into froth, visibility affected by spray
12	hurricane	64 and above	12 + (40 +)	air filled with foam and spray; sea entirely white, visibility seriously impaired

FREEZING SPRAY CHART

This chart shows the rate of icing accumulation for different wind speeds and air temperatures. Icing conditions for vessels heading into or abeam of the winds are as follows:

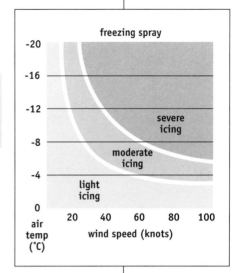

light icing	less than .7 cm accumulation per hour
moderate icing	accumulations of .7 to 2 cm per hour
severe icing	accumulations greater than 2 cm per hour

Example: *when the winds are 50 knots and the air temperature is -10°C severe icing can be expected.*

When moderate icing is expected in a forecast region it will be mentioned within the text of the forecast. When severe icing is expected a "Severe freezing spray" warning statement will be added after the wind warning as well as a comment about freezing spray being made in the forecast text.

REFERENCES

Environment Canada publications
    Coastal Weather for the British Columbia Mariner CD-ROM
    The Wind Came All Ways OWEN S. LANGE
    Marine Weather Hazards Manual

Oceanography of the British Columbia Coast RICHARD E. THOMSON

The Outer Shores EDITED BY GEOFFREY G.E. SCUDDER AND NICHOLAS GESSLER

The Stratosphere LABITZKE AND VAN LOON

Sensitive Chaos THEODOR SCHWENK

Spacious Sky RICHARD SCORER AND ARJEN VERKAIK

Heart of the Raincoast ALEXANDRA MORTON AND BILLY PROCTOR

Nootka Sound HEATHER HARBORD

Queen Charlotte Islands NEIL G. CAREY

The Last Great Sea TERRY GLAVIN

Exploring the North Coast of British Columbia
    DON DOUGLASS AND RÉANNE HEMINGWAY DOUGLASS

appendix

The Khutzeymateen Grizzly Bear Sanctuary is Canada's first and only grizzly bear sanctuary. The park, which is a little way northeast of Prince Rupert, was established in 1984 to protect grizzly bears, their habitat, and the cultural values and traditional activities of the Gitsi'is people.

PEOPLE WHO SHARED MARINE WEATHER KNOWLEDGE

Mia Algarvio, Dave Anderson, Jeff Ardron, Dewrick Arnet, Peter Barratt, Bill Beldessi, Charlie Bellis, Alice Berge, Steve Berge, Carl Botel, Tony Botel, James Bray, Robyn Brown, Doug Burles, Barry Campbell, Cyrl Carpenter, Jennifer Carpenter, Dave Chauvin, Mike Cyr, Mason Davis, Joel Eilertsen, Darrel Enger, Clay Evans, Bob Gardiner, Lou Glentworth, Bruce Grant, Mike Green, Sandy Grey, Tom Grey, Peter Grundmann, Jim Hadley, Buford Haines, Peter Hamel, Bob Hansen, Tina Hartel, Margo Hearne, Bill Hickman, Leigh Hilbert, Harry Hole, Sharla Hole, Magnus Hopkins, Gary Housty, Grant Howatt, Andy Howell, Doug Kerley, Ed Kidder, Gary Kollmuss, Matt Lawson, Larry Lohnes, Bill Mackay, Fred Mather, Sean Mather, Alexandra Morton, Raif Moss, Mike Mullin, Natalie Nelson, George Newson, Steve Oakes, Butch Olney, Norm Ostron, Wayne Podlasly, Billy Proctor, Ted Raynor, Francis Robinson, Jack Robinson, Lenny Roh, Cynthia Rose, Dennis Rose, Barb Rowsell, Keith Rowsell, Reno Russ, Doug Sharkey, Richie Shaw, Calvin Siider, Dave Siider, Ron Sine, Wayne Sisons, Peter Skilton, Nick Smith, Nancy Sparks, Wedlidi Speck, Percy Star, Al Tite, Dan Wakeman, Al Ward, Terry Wedmedyk, Mike White, Tony Wold, Ken Wright, Al Zittlau.